RETURN TO MOUNT ARARAT

or

THE EDUCATION OF NSHAN

A Living Novel

BY H. H. HAIG

VANTAGE PRESS
New York / Washington / Atlanta
Los Angeles / Chicago

Published by Vantage Press, Inc.
516 West 34th Street, New York, New York 10001

Printed in the United States of America
Standard Book Number 533-04273-9

Library of Congress Catalog Card No.: 79-63519

DEDICATED

to the memory of two million Christian Armenians
massacred by the Turkish government and people
1877-1922

Cilicia

When the doors of hope are opened
And the winter has fled away from our land,
O beautiful land of our Armenia,
When its sweet days shine forth
When the swallow returns to the nest
When the trees put on their leaves,
I wish to see my Cilicia,
The country that gave me the sun.

I saw the plains of Syria,
The mountains of Lebanon and its cedars.
I saw the land of Italy,
Venice and its gondolas.
There is no island like our Cyprus
And indeed no place is more beautiful
Than my Cilicia,
The country that gave me the sun.

There is an age in our life
When all desires come to their end,
An age when the soul
Aspires to its memories,
When my lyre becomes cold
Giving a last "hello" to love.
I wish to fall asleep in my Cilicia,
The country that gave me the sun.

—*Nahabed Roussinian*

Contents

RETURN TO
MOUNT ARARAT

CHAPTER 1

The Vista of Paradise

The French Fabre liner *Britannia,* having made excellent time from her home port of Marseilles, was now idling off the waters of the port of Providence, Rhode Island, waiting for the precise moment to enter it, to discharge her passengers at the U.S. immigrant examination station. I had chosen this port of entry rather than Ellis Island, because I had heard in Beirut that entry here would be more expeditious.

It was October 3, 1922. Early in the morning, as *Britannia* carefully headed toward the port, the sight was unbelievable—at least to my eyes. The bright sun that I had been accustomed to in the Near East now resembled a reddish orange disc in the sky. I wondered to myself: Is this the way the sun shines in America? Then I realized that the vapor, fumes, soot and smoke from the petroleum refineries prevalent in the area were playing a trick on me.

We went through the routine. Verification of official documents, physical examinations, tests for literacy, shower baths, steaming of clothing by immigration personnel, and so on. And then we finally emerged onto the street, free immigrants. A cherished dream that had its roots in the fall of our native city of Marash, Cilicia, to the Kemalist *chétés* (guerrillas) in February 1920. At long last, after a brief stay

1

in Syria, we had arrived in America, the land of milk and honey!

Two White Russian naval officers whom I had befriended aboard the *Britannia* hailed a horse-drawn carriage and, waving good-bye, went on their way. I, too, hailed a carriage. We got into it: father, mother, three brothers—the youngest one and a half years old,—and a sister, with our several suitcases and bags.

"To the railway station, please," I said to the driver. Passing through some picturesque streets, we finally reached the station, perhaps in fifteen or twenty minutes. There I bought the necessary tickets and was informed that the next train to Albany would leave in two hours.

We had some time on our hands, so my younger brother and I explored the area around the station. We bought some fruit for the family, a copy of the *Providence Journal,* and returned. Finally, the locomotive bell began excitedly to announce the imminent departure of the train. It was already dark outside. The trainman's last call and last-minute arrivals. Then the locomotive began to move forward slowly. We were on our way to Troy, New York, our final destination . . .

Father was a priest of the Armenian Orthodox Apostolic Church, representing the twenty-first generation of priests in the family, a graduate of St. Paul's Institute in Tarsus and the Marash Theological Seminary. He had been invited to become the parish priest of a small Armenian Church in Green Island, serving the Armenians of the capital district; Albany, Watervliet, Troy and Schenectady.

We were all very excited as the train approached Albany. After many trials, tribulations, unexplainable sufferings, and indeed, stark encounters with death itself at the hands of the Turks, we were here, in the free land of the star-spangled banner.

The train stopped abruptly. The trainman announced: "Albany! Albany! Transfer point to Troy!" It was dawn. After a short wait in the old and spacious station, we boarded the belt-line to Troy, eight miles to the north, on the east bank of the mighty Hudson. The train slowed down as it approached a bridge. On the left side, I noticed through the window a sign which read Green Island. Green Island! In a matter of a minute or two we crossed the old Delaware & Hudson Bridge into Troy. Troy, New York!

This, of course, was a smaller station, but adequate. We promptly telephoned our relatives and informed them of our safe arrival. They gave us the name and address of the parishioner who was to be our host for a few days. Within half an hour we were at the given address by taxi.

Levon, our host, a middle-aged man of indistinct features except for his large blue eyes, was a native of Marash like us. We had known his brother there, as a wealthy merchant. Levon was a rug and carpet layer for Quackenbush's Department Store.

Thus began the second day of an immigrant family of six in the United States of America. A spiritually wounded and physically exhausted family, especially the parents—yet not without some hope, ambition and determination.

America, what do you have in store for us?

CHAPTER 2

Pains of Adjustment

In less than a month we had settled down in our own rather modest flat on Seventh Avenue, off Jacob Street. We now had our own parlor suit, bedding, and kitchen necessities, and some new clothing for each member of the family—of course, all this on the deferred-payment plan.

Father was especially pleased to see bread and milk delivered to the door in the morning. Such service! Of course no such service existed in Turkey. You bought your bread at the bakery—in our case, the one in the tin-covered bazaar a few hundred feet from our house, at the foot of the eastern side of the Hittite Citadel of Marash. As for milk, this commodity was bought from the owner of a cow or goat at his or her house, or sometimes direct from the source in the street, at the convenience of the owner.

Father met with the parish council soon after our arrival in Troy; Mother with the ladies auxiliary of the church, St. Peter's Armenian Apostolic of Green Island, right across the Hudson from Troy. The bridge toll per pedestrian was the grand sum of two cents.

On October 15, Father celebrated his first mass in our little church.

The time had come—all too soon—for a sensitive, shy Armenian youth of sixteen, steeped in the puritanism of

4

Eastern Orthodoxy, to face life in a strange land. It was because of the generosity of a good acquaintance who had loaned us two hundred and fifty dollars that the entire family had been able to sail to these shores. That money had to be repaid as soon as possible, of course. Father's salary was hardly sufficient to provide the bare necessities of the household. That meant that I would go to work as soon as possible, albeit almost totally unprepared to face the world.

My first job, as helper in a grocery store, was offered by a distant relative. The store was within a couple of blocks of the Capitol in Albany. That meant that I would get up very early in the morning, have my breakfast at home, walk down to Franklin Square to catch the trolley to Albany, then take the Washington Avenue belt line to South Hawk Street. The store opened at seven o'clock.

The trolley tracks ran between the old canal and the main highway between Troy and Albany, on the west bank of the Hudson. I remember that sharp bend in Watervliet after one crossed the bridge over the canal. An overhead sign read Dead Stop. (My amateur translation was that the trolley stopped there out of respect for a fatality on the spot!)

The proprietor tried to teach me the abc's of the business. I was not a reluctant learner, although truthfully, I could not foresee a business career for myself. Still, I did the best I could, including delivering orders to customers' homes. The Capitol Building's kitchen was one of our patrons.

This routine lasted about six months. Meanwhile, I attended night school to improve my English, and one bright morning I was hired as a buttonhole-machine operator by Cluett, Peabody & Company, the famous shirtmakers, in their North Troy (Lansingburg) plant on River Street. A compatriot had composed the following two-line poem about this company:

I don't care if I have a $1000 debt
If only I have a job at Cluett

5

Now my working hours were much shorter, and take-home pay considerably more. A fellow worker, a neighbor, drove me and another man to the plant in the morning. On August 2, 1923, the driver passed on to us the sad news of President Harding's death; he had heard it over the radio. I had followed the presidential campaign with much interest the previous fall. Our church had been the polling place in Green Island.

Being a great admirer of President Wilson, an authentic humanitarian and a truly great American, I naturally favored the Democrats. Some years later I had the pleasure of reading the following lines that he had uttered at Getteysburg, Pennsylvania, on July 4, 1913:

> Friends and fellow citizens: I need not tell you what the battle of Gettysburg meant. These gallant men in blue and gray sit all about us here. Many of them met upon this ground in grim and deadly struggle. Upon these famous fields and hillsides their comrades died about them. In their presence it was an impertinence to discourse upon how the battle went, how it ended, what it signified! But fifty years have gone by since then, and I crave the privilege of speaking to you for a few minutes of what those fifty years have meant.
>
> What have they meant? They have meant peace and union and vigor, and the maturity and might of a great nation. How wholesome and healing the peace has been! . . .
>
> But do we deem the nation complete and finished? These venerable men crowding here to this famous field have set us a great example of devotion and utter sacrifice. They were willing to die that the people might live. But their task is done. Their day is turned into evening. They look to us to perfect what they established. Their work is handed on to us, to be done in another way but not in another spirit. Our day is not over; it is upon us in full tide.

6

Have affairs paused? Does the nation stand still? Is what the fifty years have wrought since those days of battle finished, rounded out, and completed? Here is a great people, great with every force that has ever beaten in the lifeblood of mankind. And is secure . . .

Lift your eyes to the great tracts of life yet to be conquered in the interest of righteous peace, of that prosperity which lies in a people's hearts and outlasts all wars and errors of men. Come, let us be comrades and soldiers yet to serve our fellow men in quiet counsel, where the blares of trumpets is neither heard nor heeded, and where the things are done which make blessed the nations of the world in peace and righteousness and love.

Shades of Pericles' funeral oration to the Athenians for those who first fell in the Peloponnesian war more than four centuries before Christ; and such is life, and expectations— and more expectations.

In a short while I was able to buy a good bicycle and go to work pedaling my own vehicle. I was even foolish enough to pedal to Albany and back, racing automobiles and trolley cars!

It is safe to assume that there is at least one clown in every crowd. The top floor of our factory had such a one. Several years my senior and sensing that I was a recent arrival, he began badgering me from the very first day. He nicknamed me One-eyed Nish because my right eye was a glass one. Needless to say, he did not know why it was so, nor did he much care. He played pranks on me. Often he teased me and became obnoxious. One learns, in due time, to endure such foolishness and indignities, however reluctantly, as long as the stigma *FOREIGNER* is on one's forehead.

CHAPTER 3

Facing the Realities of Life

Gradually, we were getting used to life in America. The affairs of the church were progressing satisfactorily: the newly formed mixed choir was improving steadily. Indeed, it soon won first prize at an ethnic musical-festival competition at the Troy Music Hall. The physical improvements inside the edifice were now completed. New albs and supplies had arrived, as well as a new curtain for the main altar. The Sunday school was fairly well organized.

Father, in addition to being an archpriest of the Armenian Orthodox Apostolic Church, had also been deputy prelate for some years in Marash. This meant that he represented all our six churches—parishes as well as certain others in the area— to the local Turkish government. The Armenian Protestants and Roman Catholics, too, had their own representatives. Each denomination had its own national representative in Constantinople in the persons of the patriarchs of the Armenian Apostolic Church and Roman Catholics, and an ordained Armenian Protestant minister, recognized as Ethnarch. This, of course, was in conformity with the doctrine of divide and conquer as practiced by the Ottoman Empire. Thus, the Protestants and Catholics were considered as distinct *millets* (nations).

Our church, being very close in dogma to that of the

Episcopalians, had been on friendly terms with them for some time; so Father thought that it might be useful to have a meeting with Bishop Oldham of the Diocese of Albany. Finally, the appointed day came, and he went to Albany.

The meeting had lasted well over two hours. Bishop Oldham had urged Father to give him some of the more significant highlights of his personal experiences, as the shepherd of his flock. When Father returned home, he told us, "When the bishop heard what I had to tell, he was taken aback. His eyes became moist."

Of course, in those almost pastoral days, the Armenian cause had some dedicated and powerful friends in this country. Beginning with the great and messianic President Wilson—whose prophetic advice, alas, fell on deaf ears, very likely making the conflagration of World War II inevitable—it included such outstanding and good Americans as Nicholas Murray Butler, Gov. Alfred E. Smith, senators King of Utah, Walsh of Montana, Robinson of Arkansas, Swanson of Virginia, and noninterventionist senators ("Let's mind our own business, for there is much to be done here at home"), such as Johnson of California, and Borah of Idaho. (As I recall now, the latter used to pronounce the word "national" "nay-tion-al.")

The normal, slow pace of life continued. Then we were pleasantly surprised and had the pleasure of welcoming our relative Dr. Avedis and his son, Armen, to Troy. With them also came Yervant, a good acquaintance, who had been a teacher. The words exchanged were few and far between; a facial expression or a hand gesture that told volumes, and a tear or two in between. And remembrances of events—monumental events—past, for we had all gone through a veritable hell. We were the survivors of *the first genocide of the twentieth century!*

After leaving Marash, Cilicia, in 1922, they had sought refuge in Egypt for a while. And then they had been lucky enough to secure passports to the United States, days before the gates to this country were tightly shut, particularly to the Middle Easterners and southern and eastern Europeans.

Dr. Avedis was a graduate of the American University in Beirut. He was a general practitioner with a particular interest in ophthalmology. He was the one who had seen to it that I got the proper glass eye, and had instructed me how to take care of it. His son, Armen, and I were old friends. Yervant was a graduate of the Armenian Orthodox Seminary of Marash, not far from Constantinople, and was a very serious-minded person.

Since his alma mater was accredited in New York State, Dr. Avedis had no problem in resuming his practice in Troy. Yervant's case was not as fortunate. There were no Armenian schools to teach in. A compatriot offered him a job in his meat market. So the teacher became a full-fledged meat cutter in a short time.

Then something happened that shocked the Armenian community from coast to coast. One day a judge in Oregon had ruled in his court that one Mr. Cartozian was not entitled to American citizenship because he was an Asiatic. Of course those were the days when WASP rule was supreme in the United States. There were some who looked askance at Democrats—weren't they really of questionable mentality or stupid, if not subversive?—or at least less than one hundred percent Americans!

We heard later on that this man Cartozian was probably a sharp rug dealer, and the judge just did not like him. Well, competent lawyers were hired by interested parties, and the judge's opinion was finally held invalid and overruled by a higher court. Sometimes a mere sixty-year span makes quite a difference. In retrospect, I often recall the tense and charged atmosphere in which the Sacco-Vanzetti case was handled in Massachusetts, as reported in the newspapers in the 1920s, when anti-immigrant feeling was strong—as well as the Commonwealth's governor's recent laudable action to rectify or erase that stigma. Also, with some amusement one remembers the State of Tennessee's celebrated case against one John T. Scopes, a schoolteacher. The famous "monkey trial" case, as it was popularly known, was argued in a circuslike atmosphere by two towering figures, William Jennings Bryan and Clarence Darrow and pitted the Scriptures against the theory of evolution.

But, alas! in other and more important and grave cases, millenniums of sobering experiences are verily ignored. In somber truth, *c'est la vie,* as the French would say. When a Middle Easterner washes his hands of all responsibility, his easy explanation is the magic word *Kismet!*

Getting used to a new way of life and succeeding in a strange land are not easy tasks. Requirements are more than average talent, and the gifts of adaptability and flexibility (I use this last word in its derogatory sense). These traits are not usually shared by those molded in a rigid regimen.

So days, weeks and months passed and a dull routine evolved. It was an awkward, almost painful time for me. Awakening sexual feelings and an uncertain future added up to a miserable present. Work. Supper at home. After that, spend some time at Beeman Park—in those days parks were well maintained, clean, and safe—and then to night school. Armen could afford to attend day school, thanks to his father's thriving practice. Sundays to church. Movie going with Armen was my main diversion. I often dreamed of seeing my name on the screen: "Screenplay by Nshan . . . " The price of admission to a third-rate moviehouse was a thick Indian-head nickel, not even a thin dime.

By now all our debts were fully repaid, but Father's chronic asthma was making life very difficult for him. Physician's fees and prescription drugs were getting to be an important part of the family budget. The future looked very bleak indeed to me. An abject hopelessness gripped me. I felt trapped. The prospect of the family frightened me. I could see no light at the end of the tunnel. To brave a misfortune is a lot easier said than done. Like a rat deserting a sinking ship, I wanted to join the navy. The recruiting officer at the old post office on

11

Fourth Street in Troy turned me down because I was not a U.S. citizen. He did not refer to my glass eye at all—perhaps to avoid hurting my feelings.

As if by a miracle, I had been able to continue my schooling in Marash in the German orphanage for the Armenians during the deportations. This orphanage, Beit Shalom, had been established after the barbaric Turkish massacres in 1894-1895 of Armenians in almost every town and city across Turkey. In those black days, almost 300,000 innocent Armenian lives were snuffed out, not to mention the awesome economic losses suffered by countless arsons and the officially inspired pillage that accompanied them (a Turkish habit they find impossible to break to this very day).

Father and two uncles and many other relatives and neighbors were among the deportees—during the first genocide of this century (actually covering the period 1877-1921)— the genocide that the "civilized Christian" world prefers to forget or ignore. But after the deportations in Marash, and later on in Aleppo, I had continued my education in our parochial schools. So I thought that I could perhaps, by a supreme effort, prepare myself for a position in an electric power generating station, by attending the Rensselaer Polytechnic Institute here in Troy, barely half a dozen blocks away from our new flat on Ninth Street. Little did I anticipate or realize the difficulties ahead. It would have to be on borrowed money.

So one sunny morning in 1924, before the fall term began, Father and I appeared before President Ricketts of the Institute in his office in the Pittsburgh Building, with my credentials. And I was admitted to the famed engineering college class of '28!

Soon thereafter I was one of 250 or so freshmen attending lectures. My particular group consisted of students whose last names began with A through C, Albright from Albany, Aldridge from Watertown, New York, who sported a fur coat in winter—to Cappazzullo from Mechanicsville, New York. Students from many states and countries. Bader from Indiana,

Bayer and Basset I do not recall from where. Benson from Worcester, Masschusetts. An American Indian and an American-Armenian from Connecticut. One of Secretary of Commerce Herbert Clark Hoover's sons in the class of '28, too, not to mention a Puerto Rican and quite a few boys from Mexico, Central and South America—sort of a United Nations.

The change from a workaday world to academe was a most welcome one, though not devoid of surprises, pleasant and otherwise. Dr. Patterson, a blond, proud Connecticut Yankee in his mid-thirties, the professor of physics, had been my maternal uncle's classmate at Yale. Dr. Mason, professor of chemistry, a gentleman in his late sixties or early seventies, was particularly enthusiastic when the time came to lecture on the cleansing action of soap. He had done some important work in the field. It used to irk me greatly to observe several smart-aleck students—again, clowns?—making fun of him because he had to stop and catch his breath on every landing before he got to the third floor, and the lecture hall, in the Chemistry Building. Such conduct! And the lack of respect for the elderly was unthinkable to me.

Then there was Dr. Allen, head of the department of mathematics, a business-oriented individual concerned with such service clubs as the Rotary. Professors Van Velser and Graham—one with blond hair and the other brunnette and bald—graduates of the Springfield International College and pillars of the athletic department.

Finally, there was Dr. Eno, professor of English and an authentic Anglo-Saxon, with blue eyes and trimmed blond mustache. He was in his late fifties or early sixties. For some reason he took a liking to me from the very beginning. I soon found out that he was a single man, because about five weeks after the start of the term, he asked me whether I would like to clean his apartment on a weekly basis, for which task I readily volunteered. After the cleanup we used to have a steak dinner together in the apartment. From an early age, books and writing had had a great appeal for me. I had written my first ode at the age of 12, dedicated to the Armenian freedom-fighter, General Antranik. So it was not really a great surprise that one day Dr. Eno read a humorous story of mine, describing an airplane trip to the moon, before the class!

This was before Dr. Robert H. Goddard's demonstration at Auburn, Massachusetts, of the practicality of rockets. A French doctor named Coué was preaching his doctrine of earthly salvation: "Every day, in every way, I am getting better and better. . ."

In due time we had to listen to a lecture on hygiene by a physician from the Springfield International College, quite worthwhile. Soon preparations were under way for the foot-ball season, that year's major rival being none other than Harvard U! Some weeks later, I found myself boxing on our gymnasium floor with a South American classmate. The two minutes were some of the longest in my life. Such a barbaric practice! I understand the gymnastics for youngsters to develop their bodies and as introduction to society, but in a college. . .

Also very important on the agenda was the celebration of the Institute's centennial, which was properly observed in due course on its ample and particularly suitable grounds and recorded on Movietone News reels.

Upperclassmen, especially the sophomores, were eagerly awaiting the initiation rites, particularly the "hazing" process (to this day students are maimed or killed in the observance of this barbaric ritual). Classmate Bassett hounded me over the telephone to be sure to attend. Anticipating that life on the campus would be made miserable for me otherwise, I did. It took place one evening on Seventh Avenue between Fulton Street and Broadway, where the Troy High School had been barricaded. Verily, a grand time was had by all except naive souls like myself.

After homage had been paid to tradition, students and faculty members who cared to attend were treated to enter-tainment, a soiree appropriate for the occasion. Germania

Hall and its balcony on River Street were packed with an eager crowd.

The MC, a young man in his late twenties, in his black tuxedo and with microphone in hand, proved to be a glib and apt leader, and teller of risqué jokes. Two young women, "dressed" for the occasion, did their best with songs and dances to please their mostly youthful audience. Before the evening was over, it was clear that a Miss Eckert, the tall and blonde and voluptuous one, was the star of the show. An upperclassman from the third row, with king-size penis in hand, attempted to charge toward the performers. An assault on the stage was narrowly averted.

CHAPTER 4

Coming Events Cast Their Shadows Before

So weeks and months passed, registering but slow progress. Father's health showed no basic improvement, but retrogression. The family physician, Dr. Avedis, was doing all he could to help, but his prescribed medicines proved less than effective. Then he suggested that a move to a warmer, drier climate—say, to Phoenix—might prove helpful. Given our financial condition, that was, of course, out of the question . . . All I could do was to work in the summer months in Albany in a market on Central Avenue to help.

In the meantime, Calvin Coolidge was presiding over the destiny of the country, and the country was keeping cool, going in no special direction, obviously enjoying laissez faire. The President, however, cautioned the people; a stroke of genius, that: "when more and more people are unemployed, unemployment results." The premise was self-evident, but few paid attention.

I was very much interested in the domestic and foreign affairs of my new country. The label "conservative" could be put on the vast majority of the country's daily, weekly, or monthly papers and magazines. *World's Work, U.S. News and World Report, Saturday Evening Post, Liberty, Collier's* and the *Literary Digest* (whose demise was due to a scandal, some thought) all sang the same song, so to speak. My type of magazine, such as *The Nation* and *The Progressive,* were held in general contempt—then as now. And today, *Mad, Hustler* and *Playboy* are among the most widely read. That is a message of sorts, loud and clear.

Where else but in Chicago was published "The Greatest Newspaper In the World," the *Chicago Tribune.* The *Christian Science Monitor* had chosen, with good reason, Boston as its earthly abode. The "Big Apple" was the gossip-mongering *Daily Graphic*'s home. Ditto the *Daily News*'s and the dull and staid *New York Times*'s, which never did nor does it now publish "All the News That's Fit to Print." Being a news hound, I and immigrants like myself keep reading it. (I now know, after well over fifty years of experience, that that name is a misnomer. Its appropriate name, I submit, would be *Jewish-American Times,* or *American-Jewish Times.*) Of course, the city's best daily of the times—informed, progressive, courageous—was the *New York World,* long since deceased, one of the very best in the entire country, indeed in the world.

It was something of a surprise for me to discover that Levon, the rug and carpet layer, had in fact been a bona fide ordained Protestant minister. A graduate of the Hartford Seminary Foundation, he had also attained an excellent mastery of the English language, much better than that of most immigrants. A man of unbending principles and a resolute foe of hypocrisy—a disease rampant among diplomatists and statesmen, famous and infamous—his sermons more often than not had irked members of his congregation, especially the well-to-do. They were the very antithesis of the syrupy sermons preached by such noted clergymen as Norman Vincent Peale and his ilk, who are held in high esteem by the Establishment. Levon had castigated, without fear or favor, wrongdoers and violators of the principles of justice and decency on all levels of society. To be true to his own principles, he had stepped down from his pulpit and decided to earn his bread by honest labor.

Armen and I liked him for another reason. He had been an eyewitness and participant in the forty-five days of unequal and triumphant self-defense of the Zeytoonites in December 1895-January 1896. "Believe me," he would repeat, his eyes sparkling, "these lines are true as the Gospel. I know. Yes, I was there!"

We are natives of bold Zeytoon,
And we have many a brave son;
Of our adversaries we have no fear!

In order to augment his income to support his family, Levon had mastered the art of candy making, selling his products to friends and acquaintances. So once in a while, Armen and I used to stop at his home to purchase some of his products. One day he casually suggested that we go see a parade the coming Saturday morning in Albany, also promising to tell us in some detail the heroic—I almost said epic—story of Zeytoon at some future time.

The weather was bright and warm that Saturday, and we hurried on the bus to Albany. The sight on North Pearl Street was unbelieveable: a huge parade by the Knights Templars, garbed impeccably in their regalia of sabers, red fezzes with black tassles, and mounted on well-groomed horses. The Cyprus Lodge representatives outdid them all! And there, in one float stood a man garbed as the priest Ghevond, standing erect, a silver cross in his right hand held high in the air.

This last scene was, of course, to commemorate the first war for religious freedom by the first people to accept Christianity as a state religion: that by the Armenians against the mighty empire of Persia. "From this belief no one can move us, neither angels nor men; neither fire nor sword, nor water, nor any other horrid tortures . . . " This was the reply the Armenians had sent to the Persian emperor.

The Armenians were led into battle by Marshal Vardan and Priest Ghevond on May 26, A.D. 451. Forty thousand against three hundred thousand, plus thousands of horses and trained elephants were involved in this great conflict. The Armenians lost the battle, but not their religion. History, anyone? History and historians, phew!

18

It turned out to be a memorable day for us. Soon thereafter Levon kept his promise and gave us a brief eyewitness account of Zeytoon's victory over the Ottoman Empire before the dawn of the twentieth century.

"Zeytoon, ah, a true eagles' aerie, her epical history has yet to be written!" he sighed, barely restraining his pride in this truly historic feat. "This was our Armenian-Cilician Marathon! Like Marshal Foch two decades later, they said: *Ils ne passeront pas!*" What an exhilarating story, what bravery and daring! Indeed, a greater exploit than that at the Alamo "in 1836 by the Texans, Jim Bowie, David Crockett and Sam Houston."

He referred to the fact that heroic Zeytoon and the surrounding Armenian villages had refused to bow their heads and surrender to the Ottoman Empire during the massacres of that infamous period. Nor was this the first such defiance of the brutal oppressors by this proud people. Let's look at the events in sequence as seen firsthand and told by Levon:

"Having heard of the massacres in Marash and entire Cilicia and throughout Turkey, the four princes of Zeytoon, Sargent Nazareth and the abbot of the monastery at Frnouz, Bartholomew sent an ultimatum to the commander of the Turkish barracks—built by Abdul Hamid II up in the hills some years earlier—to surrender promptly. The entire population of the surrounding Armenian villages had already taken refuge in Zeytoon.

"Imagine, if you will, this lion-hearted abbot, mounted erect on his white steed, cartridge belts crisscrossing his shoulders, and a rifle in his right hand, leading his men to battle. The scene changes. Now Abbot Bartholomew is presiding over negotiations for the Turks' surrender. His terms are met. While a diligent photographer is taking pictures, the Turkish officers, soldiers and their wives file out of the main gate of the barracks, where the abbot on his white steed, in his clerical garb, a silver cross on his chest, and a sword held high over the disarmed captives' heads, who now bow before the flag of Zeytoon, and as they are led, saying, *'Eh Wallah'* ('with

19

God')! This was certainly the most heart-warming occurrence since the fall of the Armenian fortress in the town of Gaban in 1375, when the Armenian tricolor—red, blue and orange— was hauled down for the last time.

"Then the prisoners of war were quartered safely, under the watchful eyes of Zeytoonite women. We captured 120,000 rounds of ammunition, two krup cannons, 600 Martin rifles, 170 shells, and much booty from the barracks.

"Well, the story is a long and precious one. This is material for an epic motion picture. The Turks had an army of 110,000: 40,000 regulars and 70,000 irregulars (*bashibozooks*), including Kurds, Turkmen and Circassians. They also had an immense amount of ammunition and 13 cannons, which fired 3,800 rounds at Armenian positions. We had 6,000 fighters, all of them good marksmen and armed with 'made in Zeytoon' rifles. Skilled gunsmiths, we mined our own iron ore and producd the finished product. Turkish lead from bullets was retrieved, since there was a severe shortage of lead, and refashioned as Armenian bullets.

"In Europe sympathy had developed in favour of our brave mountaineers, who had challenged the Ottoman government in defense of their liberty and went on fighting successfully for two months. The British and French ambassadors in Constantinople demanded that Sultan Hamid stop the war.

"Commander Ethan Pasha, after evaluating the situation, reported his findings to the Sultan, suggesting the termination of the conflict. On December 28, Hamid asked the European ambassadors to intervene and establish peace between the Turks and the Zeytoonites. On January 5, 1896, a Turkish soldier with a white flag brought a telegram to Zeytoon, dispatched by the European consuls—Russian, French, Austrian, British, Italian and German—in Aleppo. The 'mighty' Ottomans had failed to subdue the 6,000 brave Zeytoonites! A fifteen-point agreement was soon reached between the consuls and the Armenians; the first point stated that the six Hunchakian (members of a political party) revolutionaries, guests of the town, would *not* be turned over to the Turks."

History, anybody? What the Turks could not accomplish by force of arms, they achieved some years later, thanks to the chicanery of our European Christian brethren, as will be seen later.

As a nine-year-old Armenian boy, I had seen the scars of that patriotic war with my own eyes. A gaping hole in the roof of a monastery not far from Zeytoon, blasted by Turkish cannon fire . . . I also recall very distinctly a Turkish vegetable dealer in our neighborhood who had gone to Zeytoon in hopes of bringing home a couple of Zeytoonite maidens and returned home with one leg missing.

Armen knew little about the area. Yet my family used to spend our summer vacations in a small Armenian village. Our host, Garabed, had been one of the heroes of the war; his wife, gracious, delicate Anoush; and son, Gaboudag, somewhat younger than myself. One-hundred-and-twenty-five year old David, healthy and childlike. And older women, their headgear bedecked with medallionlike golden ornaments. Fond and dear memories that I cannot forget, ever . . .

Armen, too, was much interested in the story he had just heard. "By gosh," he exclaimed, "I will study their history and write about it." He had made up his mind to take up literature as his major course of study.

Occasionally, we used to have dinner at home with Dr. Avedis and son, and Yervant, and discuss the events of not so long ago. Yarvant had lost his pregnant wife, Mary, and two beautiful daughters, Anais and Armenouhi, during the massacres in Marash in 1920. His efforts to trace their disappearance—he himself had been in a different part of the city—had been of no avail. Their memory was ever present in his mind. His case, of course, was not at all unique; there were many other such. Dr. Avedis' family had been wiped out, too, except for his son Armen. Turkey, despite her barbaric past and unrepentant attitude, was being wooed by Christian Europe and America for sordid and selfish reasons. It is difficult

21

to explain away such conduct when you yourself have been the victim of such barbarity . . .

Father's health was deteriorating rapidly. At the end of the term I quit school and got a job in a meat market in Albany. I enrolled in a home-study course in electrical engineering and radio to continue my technical education. It seemed the only course open to me, and I applied myself to the task with great resolve. It was then that while working in Albany one Saturday afternoon I learned through an extra edition of the local newspaper of the triumphal flight of Charles A. Lindbergh to Paris!

Just about five months later, on a Saturday morning as I was about to leave the house for Albany, Mother asked me to see Father before I left. I walked into his bedroom. He touched and caressed me. When I returned home late that night, his body had already been removed to a funeral home. It had been exactly five years and seven days since our arrival in the U.S.A.

Archbishop Tirayre, the Primate, a native of Karabagh, eastern Armenia, presided at the burial ceremonies. The requiem mass was solemn and his eulogy eloquent, with brief and meaningful references to Father's life in Marash. The anointment ceremony adhered strictly to the rules and customs of the church, culminating in the final rites at the cemetery before a large number of parishioners. The archbishop wrote the Armenian epitaph, for the tombstone, which stands today in the Elmwood cemetery in East Troy.

At the close of the ceremonies, a distant relative took me to a quiet corner of the cemetery and unceremoniously advised me that I now was the man of the house, and could therefore frequent brothels, as though I were exempt from the trials and tribulations of early manhood common to all. Some men's—and women's—insensitivity knows no bounds or limits.

CHAPTER 5

Hopes and Expectations

By Thanksgiving Day 1927, we had settled down in the Brightwood (workingman's) section of the beautiful city of Springfield, Massachusetts, on the east bank of the Connecticut River. I had been offered a job at the American Bosch Corporation plant, manufacturers of radio receivers and automotive components. It was the former firm of Robert Bosch, which had been confiscated by the United States during World War I. I started out as an assembler of cone loudspeakers for radio receivers. In those days the word "stereophonic" was not yet dreamed of.

The net result of the move was that my weekly income was boosted by about 25 percent while my working hours were diminished by over one-third. Prospects for the future seemed brighter. My younger brothers and sister began to attend the neighborhood public school. My home studies were progressing satisfactorily.

The next year I was promoted to the position of inspector on the receiver assembly line. A short while later, to that of tester of power packs. Soon I was assigned to the engineering staff as a laboratory technician. That was the year that Hazeltine's neutrodyne radio receiver was superseded by Major E.H. Armstrong's superheterodyne circuitry. The transition was not really a difficult one. These advances were primarily due to deFortest's pioneering work on the audion vacuum tube. Like "no cigar, no Steinmetz," one might say, "no audion, no radio."

Nineteen twenty-eight was memorable to me for more than one reason. I received word from Troy that naturalization ceremonies would be held for a number of alien residents on Thursday morning, May 31, in the chamber of the Rensselaer County Superior Court. My name was on that list. I made sure that I got there on time.

It is perhaps fair to note that few native Americans—and I don't mean the Indians—fully grasp the extent of the emotions such an occasion evoked in this Armenian. It was not the pomp and solemnity. In a matter of seconds, I became a free citizen of these United States of America! I was no longer a subject of the barbaric Ottoman Empire, nor its equally genuine offspring, the so-called Republic of Turkey. Now I was beyond the reach of their tentacles. I could see in my mind's eye the unjust hangings, tortures, indescribable bloodbaths . . . The first planned genocide of the twentieth century. My father had been through it all. But who remembers today Meskene, Der-es-Zor, and particularly Ras-ul-Ein, the very gates of hell . . . the burning desert of Mesopotamia? But the case of one obscure Alfred Dreyfus of the French army is remembered by all, and Dachau and Auschwitz are household words.

In a pensive yet serene mood, I returned to Springfield the same day, and resumed my work the following day. By now, I had made a handful of friends at the plant.

Of course 1928 was a historic presidential election year. The state was to elect a governor and a U.S. senator, and Boston its mayor. The stage of the Springfield auditorium was graced one evening with magnetic James Curley of Boston, Governor Ely, and Senator David I. Walsh; an enthusiastic crowd cheered their leaders. And when the results of the presidential election were tabulated, I found myself poorer by two dollars, having cast my bet on Governor Alfred E. Smith of New York.

The winter season that year in Springfield proved to be interesting and busy. There was a lecture by the noted American physicist, Robert A. Millikan, from Ohio, in the Springfield auditorium. Millikan had come to visit New England, particularly the Pionee Valley, the home of his forebears, in search of his roots. Then there was a wrestling match between "Strangler" Lewis and his challenger, Labriola, with appropriate theatrics, also in the auditorium. Other events followed.

It is a tragedy of first magnitude that theologians, philosophers and moralists have not been able over the centuries to formulate realistic guidelines for children of both sexes growing from puberty to adolescence to adulthood. Those periods are among the most difficult in an individual's life. We lived an abnormal life, actually a life of fear, in the old country. For several years I had no parental guidance. Father was deported to Der-es-zor. In such circumstances one shifts for oneself.

For the largest portion of humankind, the viviparous mammals, heterosexual experience and intercourse seems to be the norm, love a prerequisite to coitus and procreation and the perpetuation of the species. In retrospect, I marvel at the uncommon sense of the swallows which used to build their nests in spring in our ceiling over the hallway, facing the tin-covered bazaar of Boughaz-Kessen, before bringing forth their offsprings! Compare this with the conduct of some "humans" . . . The Supreme Puppeteer has designed it so.

And so, when I met Stella Anderson in her home for the first time, I fell in love with her at first sight. My ideal of a girl . . . beautiful, delicate, considerate, blond and tall.

Stella's father, a man in his late forties, a friend and an employee in the magneto department at the Bosch plant, had invited me to a garden party at his home, where I was introduced to his wife and two sons. The older one, also a blond, was about my age and was eager to show me his army surplus airplane engine in the garage. The younger one's ambition, I discovered, was to become a songwriter. He was proud to show me the lyrics and music of his very first work,

25

"Ohio." They quizzed me about my background and my interest in radio and electricity. All in all it was a very pleasant two hours, and I was surprised that I did not feel self-conscious.

Like most boys, I suffered the aches and pangs of early love after this meeting, of fulfillment beyond one's grasp. For the time being, marriage was out of the question. I was the sole support of four. However, I dated Stella quite regularly thereafter. Like me, she loved the theatre. The Court Square Theatre was our favorite. We saw Eugene O'Neill's *Strange Interlude* and musicals such as *Hit the Deck*.

My foreign accent amused Stella, and when the occasion demanded, she would gladly correct my pronunciation. Was I her Rudolph Valentino? She was the first girl I had ever kissed.

Things were proceeding rather smoothly otherwise. Herbert Hoover was now our new president, intelligent, able and a good Quaker. It soon became apparent that he would rather remain a nineteenth-century man. Then came the October 29, 1929, stock market crash that shook the country and the world. The business and corporate community was in disarray, so business activity was at a standstill. Work at the plant became a seasonal affair, and to maintain a family of five even at a minimum level became impossible. The "captains" of industry had not yet thought of diversification, so that the plants could be in operation twelve months a year.

I spent much time and effort on new inventions, such as an antiglare automobile headlight, and the like. Indeed, I patented an electric sign which was by knowledgeable critics a "work of art," but a stagnant market had no use for a new gadget. I was forced to ask my younger brother to help with the family budget, to quit school and go to work. He was naturally disillusioned, but there was no choice.

Meanwhile, instead of taking firm, affirmative actions, President Hoover flooded the country with billboard advertisements, counseling to "paint up, fix up," with the implication, even promise, that such efforts would result in "a chicken in every pot and a car in every garage." Could

26

this be the same man who took prompt, decisive action to forestall widespread disease and starvation in Europe and the Near East after World War I, seeing to it that people were provided with adequate supplies of foodstuffs, clothing, and medical supplies?

Hopeless and helpless, indeed destitute, we decided to return to Troy, almost five years after our arrival in Massachusetts. I was promised a job again in a meat market in Albany. Dejected and faltering, I mailed an emotional note to Stella, before we left Springfield, finding it impossible to bid her good-bye in-person.

CHAPTER 6

Disillusionment

The job at Albany turned out to be part-time work, Fridays and Saturdays only. And in those days, Long Island ducks were good sellers! I had urged my younger brother to enroll in a home-study course in radio and electricity, offered gratis by the Commonwealth. He did so, with good results.

Democrats nominated Franklin Delano Roosevelt as their candidate for president. With less than two dollars in our collective pockets, my brother and I took the bus one morning to Albany to welcome the Messiah, the father of the yet unborn New Deal with all its ramifications. The crowd was large and enthusiastic, as we were.

Some months later my brother was able to secure a job as a service man with a nationally known retail chain store in Schenectady. The wolf was being kept away from our door, at least temporarily. And I had plenty of time on my hands, which I spent primarily in the New York State library on Central Avenue, right across from the Capitol in Albany, as well as in the Troy Public Library. I was trying to pursue a literary career. I bought secondhand correspondence courses in "the technique of the short story," "understanding the novel," and "dramatic writing." They introduced me to some well-known writers. Well, you can lead a horse to water but you can't teach writing to someone who has not the talent. And I think

28

that most teachers would rather be able to write than teach, if they only could.

However, the pursuit of literature has been a joy. Everyone has a right to his preference; to some, baseball or golf is number one. I prefer Aeschylus to Zola. And there are jokes and joke tellers, a class by themselves, and their devotees.

Mirable dictu, I found out that Armen's short stories had appeared in a number of quality magazines, and that he had gone to Hollywood to negotiate the sale of a screenplay on the Crusades to a major studio. He had nearly completed a similar work on our heroic Zeytoon. It was my pleasure to see the finished product at the Troy Theatre two years later: *Eastward, Christendom!* "screenplay by Armen." He had not forgotten to give credit to our forefathers in Cilicia, who had materially expedited this march forward.

Another "miracle," meanwhile, had taken place. Levon had been invited by a small Armenian Protestant congregation in the village of Yettem (the Armenian word for Eden) in California to become their pastor. In order to preclude any misunderstandings Levon had clearly described the problems he had had with his former congregation. They had assured him that no such problems would arise in their church, and so he had moved west with his family. I soon wrote to inquire whether he has happy; his reply was "very." Thus began my periodic correspondence with the good pastor.

I found our good friend Yervant in a pensive, even morbid, mood. He was much agitated about the imminent admission of Turkey to the League of Nations. He could not see how a nation with bloody hands, yet unrepentant and defiant, could be admitted to a league of "civilized" nations, and particularly, "Christian" nations. Of course, hundreds, nay, thousands of church bells all across Anatolia had been stilled; churches and monasteries destroyed, desecrated or used as warehouses, the parishioners bestially murdered. Where were imaginative, resourceful American investigative reporters to expose all this? At that time I had no cogent answer, but today I *do* know. It is the hydra called "national security" or "national interest."

Yervant had written to the Secretary General of the League, Salvador de Madariaga, in the name of the old Armenian-Spanish friendship, to protest any such action. (After the fall of Armenian Cilicia in 1375, King Leon V had been extended the Spanish court's hospitality on his way to Paris.) I told him that I had done the same thing, with similar results.

And one day he snapped, repeating endlessly, "Where are they, what has become of them?" referring to his wife and children. And today, physically in good health, he is still repeating the same phrases in a mental institution in Poughkeepsie, maintained by the state.

Deceptions and tissues of lies are basic fabrics and tools of most governments, it seems to this humble citizen that it has been, and remains, the standard operating procedure (SOP). The politicians' arrogance and Godlike decisions often dictate who may live or die. A recent example? The rape of Cyprus!

I floundered on, making a bare—very bare—living. Although unqualified by temperament, I tried to sell electrical appliances. The Great Depression was very much with us, and sales were few and far between. The strain took its toll on my dear mother. I had been unable to provide a bearable standard of life for the family. The deadly disease struck her, and she was in terrible pain, beyond the help of Dr. Avedis. And in a matter of weeks she passed on, leaving the family dazed. Her funeral was simple.

In abundant measure, she had tasted the bitter cup of man's inhumanity to man, massacres, deportations, and again massacres. Her father, secretary of the Social Democrat Hunchakian Party in Marash, had been killed in the 1895 massacres. So she had grown up as an orphan. Her happiness with my father had been brief and intermittent, such as attending concerts at the Armenian Central School auditorium, special occasions at the church, our summer vacations spent among Armenian villagers, where we owned a vineyard near

30

the heroic town of Zeytoon . . . The spectre of indescribable Turkish barbarisms were indelibly etched on her subconscious.

Franklin Roosevelt's innovative acts helped the country some, but the national economy was in grave disarray. Unemployment was widespread. Hope was a scarce commodity. The Civilian Conservation Corps (CCC) and the ERA (Economic Recovery Administration) touched relatively few individuals. Prohibition ended December 5, 1933, and that meant thousands of prospective jobs, but the situation required millions invested in productive work. But that, unfortunately, proved a pipe dream.

It was reported that Henry Ford had hired goons to prevent the unionization of his factories. And in the meantime, to placate the general public, he sponsored the Detroit Symphony Orchestra. Father Charles Coughlin's Sunday afternoon addresses over the radio began to attract ever-wider audiences. One bright spot in this gloomy outlook was that the Congress passed the Social Security Act on August 14, 1935.

On the international scene, things began to liven up. Adolph Hitler and Benito Mussolini had seized power in their respective countries, bent on regaining their former imperial grandeur. Republican Spain was savagely attacked by Gen. Francisco Franco, "El Caudillo", and his cohorts, and the Republic drowned in a sea of blood. The rest is history.

When Mussolini sent his legions to Ethiopia in 1936 on a "civilizing mission," the master colonizers of Europe and even the United States made the greatest noise. All were instant converts to piety and the noble principles of justice, freedom and liberty! To read the editorials in newspapers and magazines taxed one's credulity. One almost drowned in an ocean of crocodile tears. There is no honor among thieves . . . "Judge not so that you may not be judged."

The United States, of course, had had her own prophets of "manifest destiny." Nor was T.R. a mean imperialist. With one giant leap westward, he had made the Philippines an American colony and the Caribbean Sea an American Lake.

When the *Anschluss* with Austria became a fact of life by plebiscite, certain "statesmen" were incensed. But no one bothered to ask a simple, basic question: "How did England become *Britannia Magna,* by ballots or bullets?" Japan, in turn, tried her hand at imperialism with a great leap westward into China. Americans are well versed on this topic, since we followed those events with the keenest of interest. As the gunboat *Panay* plied the mighty Yangtze at a leisurely pace, no yellow gunboats sailed the Mississippi.

A weak, ineffectual League of Nations, without an effective neutral force at its command and without United States participation, inevitably doomed us to World War II. The U.S. Senate had frustrated President Wilson's heroic efforts toward membership in the League. Yet "normalcy" soon turned to abnormalcy. The contest between the proponents of Fortress America and America Firsters on the one hand and the interventionists on the other was an unequal one. On September 1, 1939, the world hovered on the brink of catastrophe. Indeed, World War II had already started.

The demand curve for trained personnel in all categories took a healthy jump upward. One day after I applied for a position at the sprawling plant of the General Electric Company at Schenectady, I was hired, and started work on December 7, 1940. During the greater part of the war, I was a member of the staff of the Aeronautics and Ordnance Department, Building 28, where some of Charles Steinmetz's memorable experiments on high voltage had been carried out. Our section's first assignment was to assemble and wire a timing device, to assure synchronous movements of Allied convoys on the Atlantic, for safer passage. German submarines had already begun to take their toll.

Extensive renovations were made throughout the plant for rapid expansion in a goodly number of specialized fields. We had already begun to buy and build new plant facilities. The products we turned out were truly amazing—from huge turbines and giant searchlights to selsyns (small electromechanical devices used extensively by the armed services) to

32

communications equipment, amplidynes and "lighthouse" vacuum tubes, and more.

Having completed a full year of work with General Electric, they felt my prospects for continued employment seemed excellent. One Sunday morning I took the train to New York, to attend an Armenian social affair in a well-known Manhattan hall. It was December 7, 1941. Before I left the hall that evening we had heard over the radio that "East Wind, Rain," had materialized: the Japanese had attacked Pearl Harbor! We could not believe our ears, but obviously, it was true. I realized there and then that things would not be the same again for a long, long time to come. (Indeed, even today, the outlook for humankind is gloomy if not downright bleak.)

Soon armed guards were stationed at the plant gates. Employees were screened by the FBI and given identification badges in accordance with clearance levels. To augment production, a seven-day week was tried out, but soon abandoned as impractical. In a matter of months thousands of new employees were hired. With millions of Americans in uniform, unemployment in the country disappeared. Rosie the Riveter and Pat the (former) prostitute worked side by side; I am sure that the latter was happy to be able to earn an honest living.

Advertising slogans attempted to spur production. One sign, hung from the ceiling, urged to "Do More for Doolittle." In a week's time we learned the meaning of the equation "Q + Q = V" (Quality plus quality equals victory). It reminded me of Albert Einstein's famous equation $E = mc^2$ (E is a quality of energy, in ergs; m is the equivalent amount of mass in grams; and c is the speed of light, in centimeters per second). Pictures of "falling objects" (bombs) needed no explanation. Henceforth, all documents, pictures and drawings were classified as restricted, confidential, secret, as appropriate.

By now, a hate campaign was in full swing and was about to reach its peak; naturally, the gigantic struggle was between "saints" and "devils." For the most venomous editorials and cartoons, the New York *Daily News,* had no peer, on the

East Coast, in this humble citizen's view. Yet before the war it had been a staunch supporter of neutrality and a severe critic of Roosevelt's policies. It was not overly enthused about the so-called "Four Freedoms" and the Altantic Charter.

For the duration, certain phrases and sentences in the Christian Bible in this Christian nation were *verboten* on the pulpit. Such as "Let him who is without sin cast the first stone," or "Blessed are the meek, for they shall inherit the earth," and "Blessed are the peacemakers, for they shall be called the sons of God." While out on the battlefields, GI's praised the Lord but passed the ammunition. We at home kept repeating the heady slogan "The difficult we do immediately, the impossible takes a little longer."

Training green help in a hurry for exacting jobs was not an easy task for G. E., but there was understanding and cooperation. I was charged with some of the responsibility. They needed to master the assembly and wiring of prototypes of remote-control turrets for B-17's, B-29's, B-36's to be mass-produced elsewhere. Pressure to do more was great, but I was doing all I could. Building 28 had major responsibility for the development of jet engines and certain specialized electronic gear for the Navy.

One day I was named foreman of a new electronics assembly unit in the Building 28 annex employing about twenty females. This was a large room that was kept under lock twenty-four hours a day. Entrance was limited to the employees of the room exclusively.

Soon special equipment arrived and was set up for operation. A professor of chemistry from the University of Colorado and his assistant were charged with its operation. Little did I realize at the time that this was a mass spectrometer for measuring U-235 concentration, a part of Gen. L. R. Groves's Manhattan District Project, perhaps the beginning of G.E.'s Knoll Atomic Laboratory. This was obviously part of the atomic bomb project. It is said that about a hundred people in the entire country were privy to it—*not* including Harry S. Truman.

My local selective service board in the Hendrick Hudson Hotel never bothered to call me during the war, obviously thinking that I would be more useful where I was than in uniform. Belatedly I commend them for their sound judgment, or perhaps my glass eye had something to do with it. In any event, I enrolled as a private in the New York Guard, Second Regiment, headquartered in the Troy Armory on Fifteenth Street. I was assigned to the headquarters and service company. By that time I had already received my F.C.C. license, radiotelephone first class, and amateur radio operation ticket, technician class. I was promoted to the rank of technical sergeant.

On the fourth of July we paraded in Mechanicsville, which has a large Italian population, perhaps because Italy was a member of the Axis. At that time we were unaware that the West Coast Japanese had already been "relocated," some say herded into concentration camps.

Armen had no valid reason for deferment. He had returned from California and was soon classified and drafted. Before he left for Camp Drum, he gave me a copy of his screenplay on heroic Zeytoon. After I said good-bye and wished him Godspeed, we shed a tear or two, for we both knew full well that his destiny was now in the hands of war gods; whether or when or in what condition he would return, no one could say... All we knew, in due time, was that his destination was the Pacific theatre.

Well, the disaster at Dunkirk in 1940 was followed by D-day in June 1944 and V-E day in May, then unconditional German surrender. Surrender offers by Japan were circulated in the newspapers, reportedly made through the Swedish embassy in Tokyo. This remains shrouded in mystery to this day. Harry S. Truman ordered the dropping of the available two atomic bombs on two Japanese cities early August 1945. Justification for this act: to save human lives. *All* governments have "justifications" for any grave act they commit.

"Do unto others..." The genie, at any rate, was out of the bottle, with unimaginable portent for humankind, well over thirty years after its first use. Mankind has truly reached a nuclear point of no return, but how many today understand its full implications, or give a damn?

Peace rumors persisted, and finally it was made official in mid-August 1945. The news reached G.E. headquarters in Schenectady early one afternoon. Everyone was delirious! At last bloodshed and destruction had come to an end! The entire plant was shut down completely for the day. In an overcrowded, dilapidated bus I reached Troy in a near frenzy.

CHAPTER 7

To Cold War—Not So Gingerly

My fear of unemployment after the conclusion of the war soon vanished. Building 28 received captured Nazi war materiel with the swastika stamped on it for examination and evaluation. I soon found out that there were two spent, or used, V-2 rockets. General Electric had decided to establish a guided missiles development laboratory on a knoll on the western outskirts of the city, above the Delaware & Hudson railroad tracks, opposite the Campbell Avenue plant. It consisted of two sections: electroncs and mechanical. I was assigned to electronics.

In the mechanical section there was one ubiquitous and attention-getting Harry Feltman. In his middle thirties, he had an unusually large head for a man who was only five feet five inches tall. Clipboard in hand, Harry took the measurements of the missiles which were being built as a national effort under the direction of a Studebaker Automobile Company executive. Soon extensive test facilities were developed in Saratoga County. A crew of about twenty engineers and technicians was maintained at the White Sands Proving Grounds, under "Pappy" Height and the general supervision of the U.S. Army Ordnance Corps. The job was challenging and I was glad to be a small part of it. Projects were code named Atlas, Hermes, and the like. The army loves exotic names from Greek mythology.

We often drove directly to the test site from our homes, to conduct, "dry" and "hot" test runs on the completed rockets from our blockhouse. During one such test, a certain component failed, and the liquid oxygen caught fire. This was long before "solid" fuels were developed. The test tower became an inferno. Thousands of hours of painstaking work went up in smoke. It lasted a few short minutes, but it seemed like a miracle that certain electronic components in a black-painted aluminum can came through unscathed! This reminds me of a launch at White Sands that was depicted as successful on national TV network, although it had actually fizzled out after the initial takeoff. This, of course, was TV magic, pure and simple, which gets weirder by the year. No one said a word about it in the laboratory . . .

Thus a firm foundation was being laid for the military-industrial complex, which becomes more influential in the highest government echelons with each passing year.

One evening I received a telephone call from New York City. It was from Armen, calling from a midtown hotel! He had just arrived from the Pacific and was planning to spend a couple of days in town. I hurried to the big city the next day, to welcome him back home. We had a hearty handshake. He seemed to be as vibrant as ever. Vibrancy and gregariousness were his main characteristics. I took him to a good restaurant. We had a couple of drinks, and we talked and talked. He talked about Okinawa and Kwajalein. He had been sent to the atoll in connection with a special army project. I soon found out that it had to do with an A-bomb test.

After some months, however, it became apparent that his health was being sapped with each passing day. His vitality diminished gradually but not his genialness, his bright, cheerful outlook. His father took him to a specialist for a thorough diagnosis. The verdict was leukemia, but Armen was never told the truth. The consensus was that he had been stationed too close to ground zero during the test. To set radiation tolerances, and build and calibrate precision instruments is not an easy task, even today.

Armen died a year after his return. His funeral was private, with only close friends attending. He was interred in Elmwood cemetery, and with him went a great future in literature. Yet today we have more warmongers, even after Korea and Vietnam, than ever before. Armen's father followed him to his grave a relatively short time thereafter, an early death that he himself had predicted.

Deutschland uber alles. Drang nach Osten. Lebensraum, A thousand-year Reich. Britannia rules the waves. The sun never sets on the Union Jack. We are number one! We, the Israelites, are number 1 in the Middle East!

It is amazing how man, the so-called rational animal, persists *not* to profit from past mistakes. The urge of one nation to have dominion over all others persists. The goal of a free Parliament of the World seems to be as elusive as ever. Europe, especially the Soviet Union, and a goodly portion of Asia were devastated and in shambles after World War II. But who shall dominate the United Nations and use it to promote its own interests? That was the really important question of the day. Had FDR lived several years longer (his was most certainly an untimely death), would the ugly events, the postwar anti-Soviet hysteria for which Truman turned out to be such a pushover, be significantly different? That is one sixty-four-dollar question that cannot be answered with any degree of certainty.

The OSS (Office of Strategic Services) under Gen. Bill Sullivan—known as the cloak-and-dagger boys—was transformed into a government within a government, accountable precious few knew to whom. The myth of "politics stops at water's edge" was propagated. But in due course, Patrice Lumumba, Mohammad Mousadag, and Salvador Allende Gossens, were "eliminated" or toppled from power by the scum of their own societies. Long live freedom and democracy! Then one of the most arrogant men ever to walk on this globe, the architect of the Gallipoli disaster in World War I exuding contempt for others and dominance from every pore in his body, an unrepentant, dyed-in-the-wool imperialist (and at the same time would-be champion of freedom and liberty) appeared on a Fulton, Missouri, rostrum with his ringing, infamous "Iron Curtain" speech. The true meaning of this speech was that his aim was to institute or erect a *cordon sanitaire* around the Soviet Union, like the French goal to isolate Germany after World War I. The inexplicable part of the whole charade was that the American people swallowed all this patently absurd balderdash, hook, line and sinker. And with gusto. No doubt, thanks to the shrill yellow press.

"I did not become His Majesty's prime minister in order to preside over the liquidation of the British Empire!" Consider who was talking about "curtains." The master curtain-maker himself! The construction of the Cairo-Capetown railway was ordained by the Lord himself, of course; but not that of Berlin-Baghdad. Bent on preserving ill-gotten gains, Churchill never bowed his head before the tombs of Mohandas K. Gandhi and Jawaharlal Nehru. This, I submit, is human indecency carried to the nth degree.

Henry Luce declared this, the twentieth, the American Century. And things have never been the same. The frosty highway to the Cold War battlegrounds remains the same. And it is ever so easy to manipulate public opinion. You need not have a Goebbels to do the job.

Events proceeded at a maddening pace. God said, five millennia ago: "Let there be light." "And there was Light!" (Please see the Scriptures.) Harry S. Truman (the "S" stands for nothing) of Independence, Missouri, a cum laude graduate of the Pendergast machine in Kansas City, spoke thusly: "Let Greece and Turkey become North Atlantic countries." And lo and behold, they *did* become North Atlantic countries, and the NATO chain was completed. Il Duce's *mare nostrum* became an American lake. The Iskenderun-Kars military road in Turkey, from the Mediterranean to the Soviet border, was built posthaste by American dollars and under American supervision; and A-bombs were brandished at foes, real or imaginary.

The dapper Dean Gooderham Acheson, in matchless splendor, was also "present at the creation." Our proconsul Gen. Douglas MacArthur reigned supreme in Tokyo. Remember: "There is no substitute for victory"? Still, Korea remains a problem for the world, since Truman's "police action" failed to solve the problem. The human animal is a slow learner, and similar errors have been repeated, with compound interest in blood and treasure.

Then appeared on the scene the indefatigable, peripatetic John Foster Dulles, seized with a righteous zeal which he later transformed into a pactomania (the last of which was SEATO, ungloriously buried not too long ago) while his brother, Alan, practiced the bizarre, occult, "Craft of Intelligence." Someone handed me the following two lines re this relationship:

When Dulles brothers are in charge
The ship of state is in good hands . . .

An American general, whose parents had been dismayed at his selection of the military as a career, who had no profound understanding of world history or management of government,—unlike Woodrow Wilson—was elected president of these United States. Adlai Stevenson was rejected by the electorate; the plethora of flag wavers had triumphed.

The very durable, indeed perennial, J. Edgar Hoover—a resolute foe of liberal, progressive thought—was in firm control of the domestic scene, though the influence of the underground seemed to grow each passing year. In the meantime, Hoover apparently basked in the reflected glory of such radio programs as *Gang Busters* and *The FBI in War and Peace*. And the country was immobilized in the grip of McCarthyism.

The climate in the Capital District in New York State is usually very severe in winter, and I was sick and tired of commuting to Schenectady daily. My two younger brothers

41

were now living in Sea Girt, New Jersey, where the climate is milder. So I applied for a position as an electronics engineer at Fort Monmouth. After an interview, I was accepted, and subsequently notified by telegram from the commanding general to report for work on a given day in early October. The year was 1952.

CHAPTER 8

Civilian Employee, U.S. Army Signal Corps

After passing the usual physical examination at Fort Monmouth, I was led to the office where I was to be sworn in as a new employee. By the Stars and Stripes stood a female officer, a Ms. Harrison, who was in charge of the ceremony. This was indeed a solemn occasion for me; it was just thirty years ago that I had landed on these shores. When I repeated the oath after her, my eyes were moist and my voice shaky . . .

The facilities at Fort Monmouth are quite extensive. Besides the fort complex itself, the camps Coles and Evans, and other facilities. Camp Coles consisted primarily of two departments, field engineering and procurement. I was assigned to the latter group. Working conditions were good, the work was interesting, and the rustic atmosphere of our site appealed to me. There was a steel tower on the hill for a microwave "dish" antenna. On a clear day one could see the Statue of Liberty and the New York skyline from the top. In a breeze the tower swayed gently back and forth.

The U.S. Army offers, gratis, a variety of technical courses to its military and civilian personnel, by correspondence from the Signal School in Fort Monmouth, the U.S. Engineer School at Fort Belvoir, and other various installations. I gladly took advantage of this opportunity, striving to keep abreast of current developments. My interest included electron tubes, transistors, antennas, pulse techniques, TV, radar and infrared technology, among others. It was something of a surprise to me that the instructor of the course on antennas, a former professor, was a GS-14, while my younger brother with only a high school education, had been promoted to GS-15 and my youngest one had been promoted to a full professorship, teaching electrical engineering at the University of Pennsylvania, and had been appointed a department head and elected a fellow of the Institute of Electrical and Electronics Engineers.

Some months later Camp Coles initiated a program of sending selected technical personnel to the U.S. Army Logistics Management Center at Fort Lee, Virginia, where similar personnel from army facilities in the eastern part of the country spent a week discussing problems of mutual concern and interest in formal sessions, as well as lectures by specialists on relevant and appropriate topics. The spring weather was excellent and Southern hospitality up to par; it was an enjoyable week well spent.

Upon my return to Camp Coles, I was told by my section chief that I had been detailed by Cololnel Parsons, chief of our installation, to act as interpreter to a group of Turkish signal corps officers, who were about to visit Fort Monmouth, among other army installations in the country. (None of the Turkish officers spoke English.)

They soon arrived. Colonel Parsons led a guided tour of selected facilities in the Fort Monmouth complex. A paper had been prepared detailing some of the army signal corps' procedures in procurement. This I translated into Turkish with great care, working late into the night in my home. Not being familiar with the peculiarities of the Roman characters now used by Turks, I used the Armenian alphabet instead, which has thirty-six characters.

On a Friday morning, we gathered in our auditorium. Colonel Parsons briefly explained the mission of the U.S. Army Signal Corps, which in essence is the research, design, development, production and procurement of signal corps materiel and the training of personnel to operate and maintain them. I then read the paper before the Turkish officers and a number of Coles personnel. A question and answer period followed.

That evening we were treated to a dinner in Scrivin Hall at the fort, plus the usual cocktails. About twelve colonels and majors were present; one American colonel had just returned from a tour of duty in Iran. One Turkish officer expressed his disappointment with American food. Another Turkish colonel delivered a message from one General Ibrahim. I was taken aback, and no American officer responded to that message, since it required the attention of much higher authority.

Seeking greener pastures, I asked for a transfer to Camp Evans, in the Shark Hills area, on and above Marconi Road in Glendola. The mission of this installation was different, the assignments were interesting and varied. Certain deficiencies had been noted in radar sets, during the Korean war due to the peculiar topography of that country, and experiments had been carried out to correct them. Several times our section tested the improved models at Fort Dix. Similar tests were conducted on improved IFF (identify friend or foe) circuitry on radar sets, and on other techniques of interest to the military.

I soon discovered that Harry Feltman's brother, Jim, was employed in my branch. At that time the papers were reporting the trial and conviction of Harry Feltman of Schenectady as a Soviet spy . . . When I made sure that Jim was *the* brother of Harry Feltman, I could not help exclaiming to my colleagues, "This is a small world!"

Senator Joseph McCarthy's savage attack on the U.S. Army was gaining momentum daily. He came to Fort Monmouth, searching for Soviet spies. The general attitude of the personnel was one of disdain. Many of us admired the army counselor Welsh for his dignity and decency. This

C. J

45

truly sad period in American history—which culminated in Vietnam—reminded me of Christ's time and the period following His crucifixion. In Palestine, Canaan, Syria, Armenia, Anatolia, Greece, Rome and Ethiopia, the damning question was: Are you now, or have ever been . . . a Christian? So, many Christians sought refuge in dungeons, catacombs, caves and cloisters . . . I kept asking myself the question, is this really the world of the wicked? The overwhelming evidence seemed to say, "Yes!"

The terrible experiences that my people had gone through, particularly during the past three quarters of the century, were clearer and more vivid in my mind's eye than ever before . . . How could such a great crime be forgiven and forgotten, and the perpetrator accepted as a bosom friend, as did Harry S. Truman? And the *New York Times*'s cavalier advice to the Armenians: "If you can't forget it, forgive it." Would this haughty newspaper give quite the same kind of advice to the Jews, regarding the Nazi crimes? Unthinkable!

France had handed over, on a silver platter, the Sanjak of Alexandretta to the Turks to placate her (where Turks were a minority) whereas a *free* plebiscite would have given it to Syria, where the heartwarming episode of Franz Werfel's *Forty Days of Musa Dagh* had taken place. The novel was an American best seller, and Metro-Goldwyn-Mayer soon bought the film rights of this epic story. But years later I learned to my chagrin that it was not produced—not because of the chicanery of the Hollywood moguls but because of the tacit opposition of the mightiest nation of the world, the United States of America!

Below is a copy of a letter from the then secretary of state to the Turkish ambassador (Münir), dated September 12, 1935:

The Secretary of State presents his compliments to His Excellency the ambassador of Turkey and acknowledges the receipt of the ambassador's note of September 5, 1935, relative to the question of the production of *Forty*

Days of Musa Dagh by the Metro-Goldwyn-Mayer Corporation.

In conformity with the telephone conversation between the second secretary of the embassy and the chief of the division of Near Eastern affairs, a copy of the ambassador's note was communicated informally to the Honorable Will H. Hays, president of the Motion Picture Producers and Distributors of America, Inc. While the department can, of course, assume no responsibility for the commitments of the Motion Picture Producers and Distributors of America, Inc., that organization has now informed the department, with reference to the ambassador's note of September 5, 1935, that "the script has not been finished and will not go into production without the approval of the Turkish ambassador." 811.4061 Musa Dagh-36

Writing to the chief of the division of Near Eastern affairs, Mr. Murray, the Turkish ambassador, Mr. Münir expressed his gratitude in the following words on October 4, 1935:

My dear Mr. Murray:

A few days ago Mr. Orr of Metro-Goldwyn-Mayer called on me at the embassy to discuss the filming of *Musa Dagh*. As a result of our conversation, he joined us to to admit that the filming of this novel, whatever modifications it might be subjected to, could not but be harmful from every standpoint.

Consequently he declared that they would rather drop this scheme altogether.

I have already informed my government of the satisfactory result reached through the kind support of the State Department.

In this connection, it is an agreeable duty for me to extend to you my best thanks and hearty appreciation for the efforts you have been so kind to extend in this matter, without which the happy conclusion which has created an excellent impression in my country could not possibly have been attained.

Reiterating my gratitude, (etc.)

Amen! "The land of the free and the home of the brave." Appeasement, anyone? And this was long before Neville Chamberlain went to Munich, umbrella in hand, to appease the German Führer. If this is not official censorship in peacetime, then what is it? Yet Hollywood produces an anti-German film at the drop of a hat! Human rights, anyone?

After much thought, I decided to resign my position and devote my full time to the cause of the deliberately forgotten genocide. I knew that this could best be done on the island of Cyprus; Archbishop Makarios was a good, sincere friend of the Armenians.

Accordingly, I resigned my position and made the necessary preparations for the voyage. I was living in Asbury Park, on Sunset Avenue, overlooking the lake of the same name. An elderly Irish couple was boarding in the same house. On Sunday afternoons, we used to stop at the Berkley Carteret bar for a couple of beers. Having learned of my resignation, the elderly gentleman had put two and two together and concluded that I had been fired as a security risk. I considered it beneath my dignity to reply in kind. I just ignored him. Now I could see how far the poison of McCarthyism had spread, how it had penetrated and permeated every level of American society . . . But the Cypriote fight for independence was reaching a climax, amid widespread violence. After some sober thought, I concluded it would be prudent to postpone my travel plans for the time being, and I decided to seek employment again.

My application to Picatinny Arsenal in North Jersey was favorably considered and I was hired as an electronics design engineer in the Atomic Applications Laboratory. This installation, which retained a large number of civilian employees, was run by the U.S. Army Ordnance Corps. It was ideally located for its purposes, nestled between high hills. Working conditions were good.

My first assignment was the design of an electronic timing device for a certain application, working with high-voltage circuitry. I almost electrocuted myself in the process. It reminded me of two narrow escapes I had had at American Bosch in Springfield, under different circumstances.

After staying at the Dutton Hotel in Dover for a while, I moved to a good rooming house. Then I began to attend morning services in the local Episcopalian Church. Wonders never cease. Harry Nightingale, who used to come to American Bosch in the late twenties as representative of a well-known radio tube manufacturer, was one of the parishioners. He was, I found out, employed in a different department at the arsenal. In due course I became a full-fledged member of the church, and this was to change my life.

In due course my clearance level was raised to Q, and I was sent to Albuquerque, New Mexico, to an army installation, for six-weeks course in elementary atomic technology. I shall call it "The Uses and Abuses of Atomic Energy." Like most people, I *do* have a fear of the unknown, and my grasp of this field is rudimentary at best. But since the first two atomic bombs were used to incinerate two cities by a Christian country, I have the most profound abhorrence for this technology.

After mulling over this matter for a while, I asked for a transfer to a different department, my wish was granted. I was sent to the branch chief's office for a briefing. Imagine my surprise! He was none other than Ivan, the blond Russian naval officer whom I had met aboard the *Brittannia* ages ago! He recognized me too. "Your are *the* Nshan I met on the boat, aren't you?" he asked, to make doubly sure.

"The very same one," I assured him.

The section chief was one Dom Arnone, a pleasant native New Jerseyan. I soon had occasion to meet two professors of chemistry on the faculty of the New Jersey College of Engineering, who were consultants to the arsenal. One was a

German named Heintz. The other, Karl, was an Austrian who had served the Third Reich in Berlin in similar capacities. Both men had survived the terrible bombing of the war unscathed. The task of our section was to determine, by electronic and other means, the strength of explosive charges, and particularly of different "mixes," since such development is a continuing process.

We were told that a group of intelligence men and women from the Pentagon was to pay a visit to the arsenal. I was charged with the responsibility of explaining our section's function. The branch and section chiefs were to be present, of course. After our guests were gone, the branch chief called me aside and commended me for a brief but essentially complete, orderly, logical presentation.

My membership in the church changed my life in a totally unexpected manner. During a social gathering, I met one Virginia Avakian (an Armenian surname). She had an extremely pleasant personality. Again, it was love at first sight for me . . . Soon I found out that she was a widow with an adolescent boy.

I began to date Virginia. We would go to a favorite restaurant of ours on Route 46, not far from Dover, every Sunday afternoon. Though born in Hartford, she spoke excellent Armenian. To demonstrate her penmanship, she once wrote the Armenian version of her first name on the napkin at the dinner table.

Her parents had been natives of Garin, in eastern Turkey, a fine Armenian city. Her husband, an internationally recognized contractor, had been killed in a plane crash two years earlier. A graduate of the Massachusetts Institute of Technology, his latest accomplishment had been the design and construction of an electrical power-generating complex for the government of India. During World War II he had done considerable work for the U.S. government. He, like myself, had been a native of Armenian Cilicia.

After a brief but hectic courtship, Virginia and I were married in our church. I then moved into her home in a fine section of the town. Our marriage turned out to be mutually satisfying, although her son, Ara, did not particularly appreciate a substitute father. We both did our best to be helpful to him in any and all ways we could.

Having settled down to a new and more rewarding life, I began to contact some of my old friends and acquaintances. Number one on the list was the evangelical preacher Levon, out in Yettem, California. Originally, Virginia had belonged to his denomination. Meanwhile, I continued to follow current events closely. The callousness and duplicity of our world "leaders" appalled me. No one seemed to grasp the true meaning of the phrase "The genie is out of the bottle . . . "

CHAPTER 9

Beep . . . Beep . . . Beep . . .

It had been a habit of mine for many years to report to work well ahead of time, so that I could read my morning paper and relax before tackling the day's task. On Friday, October 4, 1957, I was already at the test site day's assignment when Dom showed up early, too. He had a glum look on his face.

"Have you heard?" he asked.

"Heard what?"

"The Beep . . . Beep . . . Beep."

Of course I had. He was obviously refering to Sputnik I, the little ball that was circling our globe every ninety minutes or so. The shock waves that went through the country were stronger than those after Pearl Harbor, if possible. The scientific-technical community was dismayed, to say the least.

The primary reason for this surprise was that the American news media had brainwashed the American people in representing the Soviets as uncouth bullies or sadistic clowns. After Churchill's anti-Soviet outburst at Fulton, Missouri, the government's various actions seemed to be tailored to fit that psychology.

Most people tend to overlook the fact that American science is essentially only two centuries old and that its roots are primarily European. Even in the matter of language, the number of English words with Greek roots is truly amazing. The A-bomb was essentially a European achievement. And it is worth noting that one Dmitri Ivanovich Mendelyeev, a Russian, was one of the pioneers in the development and formulation of the periodic table.

Given the American temperament, John F. Kennedy's crash program to catch up and surpass the Soviet feat was inevitable. And the Cold War got even colder.

JFK's charm and charisma, his masterful use of the English language, and the Camelot atmosphere had captivated me. I thought he was the second Messiah . . . But soon my hopes were dashed. Now it all seemed like a grandiose act on the world stage devoid of substance or meaning. *"Ich bin ein Berliner!"* (Yesteryear, we were doing our level best to eradicate and obliterate Berlin.) If some observers are to be taken seriously, Kennedy was more concerned with the pleasures of the flesh and the glamor of the office than with the exceedingly difficult—indeed monumental—task of improving the human condition.

The Bay of Pigs disaster followed. Adlai Stevenson was made to look like a fool or an idiot at the United Nations. Still and all, when his death was confirmed on that Friday afternoon, November 22, 1963, I was too distraught to continue work.

I corresponded with Levon rather regularly. I asked him to mail me copies of his sermons on war and peace, justice and brutality. He obliged. In one letter he made reference to the trial and hanging of Adolph Eichmann by Israel. The Armenians, of course, had their "Eichmanns" too, in the persons of master butchers Enver, Talaat and Djemal, who engineered and carried out the first genocide of the twentieth century, and who were in fact sentenced to death as war criminals by a Turkish court after World War I. The verdicts were never carried out by the Ottoman government; it remained for Armenian revolutionaries to accomplish the task. Yet the unrepentant Turk, a bosom friend of Uncle Sam—

geopolitics makes such strange bed fellows!—pays homage to the memory of Talaat, having removed his body from his grave in Berlin and reburied it on Freedom(?) Hill in Istanbul.

Levon was as dismayed with the Vietnam War—I almost said Cardinal Spellman's war—as I was. John Foster Dulles's phony SEATO allies were conspicuous by their absence in the conflict, so we had to bring in 50,000 Korean mercenaries and 1,600 Philippine "medics." Then came the chicanery of the Gulf of Tonkin resolution, on flimsy pretexts.

The shameful overt and covert war in all of Indochina continued unabated. Demeaning activities such as search-and-destroy missions, Operation Phoenix, and "free-fire" zones were carried out with pride by "responsible" personnel. Meanwhile, brothels from Bangkok to Tokyo, Saigon to Manila, were doing land-office business as the flower of American youth sowed its oats.

And then, apparently without warning, the Tet Offensive began on January 30, 1968. This was during the imperial presidency of Mr. Baines Big, who had already crushed a progressive-liberal movement in the Dominican Republic on April 28, 1965, the pretext being the same old bromide: protection of American lives and property.

The American people were rather confused and their morale at a new low. "Think tank" experts and other "specialists" in the field proposed a countermeasure to remedy the situation quickly. On a fine morning President Big summoned a small number of selected wire service executives, columnists, and the like to the inner sanctum of the White House, where he sampled his favorite drink. He had already had several drinks before the invited guests arrived. "Gentlemen of the press," he told them, "I have an important announcement to make this morning." As the sentence was barely completed, someone brought in one of his beagles. The guests were served their favorite drinks, and a few minutes of chit-chat followed.

"I am going to christen my favorite beagle this morning, and you shall be witnesses to this solemn and grave event," the president declared. There was a polite giggle from the

54

guests. The dog approached his master expectantly, wagging his tail furiously.

"I, Darius I . . . "

"I, Alexander the Great . . . "

"I, Genghis Khan . . . "

"*I*, President Big . . . "

Addressing his pet, the president continued: "Now listen to this very carefully, do you hear me?" The dog responded with a sharp bark.

"From now on, you shall answer to the name 'Ho,' do you hear me?" the master repeated. The dog responded with a sharper bark. President Big's guests comments were a restrained laughter.

Ho Chi Minh's "crime" had been that he had defeated French colonialism in his country—as George Washington had done in this country 200 years ago vis-à-vis another colonial power—and Ho was unwilling to submit to an American yoke, just as Washington had been unwilling to submit to the English yoke.

The following day Avery Alsop wrote in his column how great a success the "Tet affair" had been for the American side. And defoliants, napalm, and bombs of all kinds took their daily toll at an accelerated rate.

On the other side of the ledger, not everyone in the country approved of this dirty war. I admired and applauded such groups as the Clergy and Laity Concerned, and the courage of individuals like Jane Fonda when they appeared. An unbelievable tragedy—indeed, a massacre—occurred at the Kent State University on May 4, 1970. And demeaning, ugly slogans such as "America, Love It or Leave It," appeared on bumper stickers. My job was losing its value and meaning with each passing day.

Honorable and brilliant men—George Washington and Thomas Jefferson, Abraham Lincoln, Woodrow Wilson and Norman Thomas, Corliss Lamont and Henry Steele Commager, not to forget a LaFollette and Pinchot—have streaked across the American firmament. Unfortunately, there are their opposite numbers: Joseph McCarthy, Richard Milhous ("I am not a crook") Nixon, George Wallace, and Curtis ("Bomb them into the Stone Age") LeMay, Barry Goldwater, and Henry Kissinger.

Under the devious Nixon administration the American political system reached its nadir. Sharp operators abounded in the White House; yet this building became the home of "breakfast prayers," and so the American people were lulled into the belief that "God is in His Heaven" and everything was under control. The breakfast prayers were little better than cheap vaudeville skits, as the Rev. Billy Bingham, a frequent participant, testified later. He and his wife had often been embarrassed at the off-color jokes they had heard at these gatherings. And Richard Nixon, himself the son of Quaker parents, refused to admit—for shame!—representatives of that sect into the White House, just to hear their plea. This is the kind of world we live in—a callous and unjust world.

A year of personal tragedy followed. Ara, my stepson, had been studying aeronautical engineering at M.I.T. but could not concentrate on his studies. He decided to volunteer for the air force. As a first-generation American, he was determined to fight for his country, and with each passing day, he became more determined to join. My wife, Virginia, a devout Christian, strongly disapproved. First of all, she thought the Vietnam war was unjust and immoral; and secondly, she firmly believed in the commandment: Thou Shalt Not Kill. My advice to Ara had to be more subtle and discreet. But he was in no mood to listen to either of us. He even thought my words betrayed disloyalty to America. He enlisted with the zeal of a first-generation American. His mother was deeply concerned.

A year later his body was sent home. He had died in an accident at the base. A fine, very considerate lieutenant from Youngstown, Ohio, represented the air force at the funeral. Six months later his mother joined him at the cemetery, dead of grief.

I immediately applied for retirement at the arsenal. The last letter I received from Levon had said:

> ... I doubt that 200 Americans out of 200 million honestly, truly believe that Vietnam was ever a threat to their safety and security, their well-being or way of life ... It grieves me to the marrow to admit that Uncle Sam has become *the* premier terror bomber of the entire world ... Suppose such bombing were ordered by a Hitler or Mussolini; what would be the reaction of the American public, if not one of just condemnation?
>
> Perhaps someone in ultimate authority, took the advice of a couple of Big Brains, or think tanks, or computer readouts, or multinationals, for this adventure ten thousand miles away from home . . . Or perhaps someone thought of transforming the Pacific Ocean into an Americus sea . . . They don't seem to understand the true meaning of the saying "The genie is out of the bottle . . . "

After the paperwork had been completed, my termination date was set for July 14 (Bastille Day), 1973. I joined a retirement luncheon with several colleagues who also retired on the same day, and a number of well-wishers at the Lincroft Inn in Dover.

The evening paper the same day reported the death of Heinz and Karl at a railway crossing accident in peaceful Morris County. Such is life.

I learned that an Armenian orphanage on Cyprus, financed by a Danish missionary group, was looking for an electronics engineer, to establish an electronics course there. I promptly volunteered.

Another well-known Armenian institution on the island, the Melkonian Institute, concerned itself with the teaching of the Armenian language and history, as well as other courses like bookkeeping, agriculture, and so forth. It had been founded in the early twenties by two Armenian bachelor brothers who had amassed a fair fortune by manufacturing Egyptian cigarettes, which were then popular in the United States.

I immediately began to procure the necessary hand tools, textbooks and instruments, such as multimeters, oscilloscopes, signal generators, transistor and tube testers, and the like. I was on my way to Cyprus within a matter of weeks.

CHAPTER 10

The Cyprus Interlude

The delightful, beautiful island of Cyprus has a certain emotional appeal for us Cilician Armenians. During the era of our kingdom in Cilicia—which was conquered by the Mamelukes of Egypt in 1375—our ties to Cyprus were often close and intimate. This was particularly true during the Crusades. On clear days, the Cilician mountains can be seen from high points on Cyprus.

I reached my destination on schedule, the monastery of St. Magar, midway between Nicosia and Krycnia. Imagine my surprise when I discovered that Father Nerses, the principal of the school, was none other than Hovannes, a native of the Armenian village of Frnouz, fifteen miles to the west of our former vineyard at Arékin and the foot of the natural twin fortresses. Below flowed the river Guredin. All in Cilicia. I knew and remembered them so well; in 1922 they had told me not to forget them. Indeed, we had sheltered Hovannes's wife in our home during the deportations.

Hovannes and Martha had already arranged a get-acquainted dinner for the following Sunday afternoon. The dining hall was filled with bright, eager Armenian boys. As is usual at such affairs, there was a good musical program. A number of the articulate boys recited patriotic poems, which I enjoyed immensely. The following are some samples:

Armenia

Armenia, the land of Paradise
You are the cradle of the human race,
You are my native motherland,
Armenia, Armenia, Armenia.

In your majestic name
My heart is inspired anew.
And anxiously I long for you,
For you, for you, O my only hope,
Armenia, Armenia, Armenia.

Small

Yes, we are small,
The smallest pebble
in a field of stones.
But have you felt the hurtle
of pebbles pitched from a mountain top?

Small
as the smallest mountain stream
storing rapids, currents
unknown to wide and lazy valley rivers.

Small,
like the bullet in the bore
of the rifle;
small as the acorn waiting to sprout.

Small
As the pinch of salt
That seasons the table

Small, yes
you have compressed us, world,
Into a diamond.

Small,
you have dispersed us,
Scattered us like stars,
We are everywhere in your vision.

Small,
but our borders stretch
from Pyuragan telescopes to the moon
from Lousakan back to Urartu.

Small as the grain of uranium that
cannot be broken down, put out, or consumed

                    Ararat

We stand rooted
eyelashless, eye to eye,
My mountain and I

Faith, they say, moves mountains
as Noah moved you into
sight

I am filled with the same fanatic
flood.
And still we are planted
stones.

I curse my own immobility
Is it for nothing?
This is Ararat, I am an Armenian,
and we are apart

For how long? Satan knows.
I am transient, I am mortal,
I shall pass

And you, my mountain,
Will you never walk toward me?

I Love My Armenia

I love the sun-bred language of my Armenia;
The sad lamenting chord of our ancient lute, I love;
The crimson splash of flowers, the intoxicating scent of roses
And the swift waist of a dancing maid, I love.

I love our somber sky, clear waters, crystal lake,
the summer sun and the howling of winds from the mountains;
The uninviting, dreary shacks, smoke-covered ceilings, walls
And the thousand-year-old stones of our ancient cities, I love.

Wherever I go, I shall never forget our mournful songs,
Nor shall I forget our iron-lettered script, our prayer;
No matter how deep, my fatherland will pierce my heart

Orphaned and bleeding with wounds, I shall love my beloved
    Armenia

For my homesick heart there is no other story,
No greater minds than Narek's and Kuchak's;
And in the entire world you will not find a mountaintop like
    Ararat's,
Like an unreachable peak of glory. I love my Mount Masis.

Oath to Ararat

We will reach your sacred peak
Once the barrage of bombs subsides,

Once the blood seas resign themselves
To being the color of blood,
Once the butchered dove of peace
Returns from the holocaust
With his olive branch,
We will reach that summit.
From every city, by road or field,
From every gutter and corner of exile,
Watch us gather, adding one to one
And rank to rank to storm
Our father's dream.
And watch the black walls with which
Fate has barricaded us
Shatter.
The ache of our hearts will lead us
Like a trumpet call,
To our lands and water.
Let the sun collapse;
Let the road lead through hell,
We will reach your peak.
Look at our numbers, swelling
Rank on rank,
Brave and burning.
Look at our hunger reaching toward you
With the grasp and reach of Vahakn.
Look at our souls, clean as your snows
And our will, hard as your stones.
God of Granite!
Holy mountain!
Believe us that we can, that
We shall reach your peak!

The enthusiasm of the students drove me to greater effort. Being a U.S. licensed radio-telephone operator first class, with radar endorsement, and an amateur radio operator, technician class, I had no difficulty setting up an amateur radio station, with the special permission of the Cypriote government

I concluded that my decision to come to Cyprus had been a wise and rewarding one. Everything was proceeding according to plan . . .

One day Father Nerses confided to me that he had been writing a comprehensive history of the noted Armenians of Cilicia since the fall of our kingdom in 1375, and that he would appreciate any memoirs, remembrances or photographs I might be able to offer towards this project. I agreed gladly. I also began preparing the following rough outline of a novel or autobiography—this had to be one for the nuclear age— that I had been planning for a long, long time:

Born in Marash in 1905 at the family home at the foot of the 3500-year-old Hittite fortress. Vague remembrances of the massacre of 1909. Father jailed unjustly by the government. Visit to jail with mother. Enrollment in kindergarten in our church, St. Stephen's, opposite my father's office.

Visit of Catholicos Sahag II of the Great House of Cilicia to our six apostolic churches in the city. Our turn had come. Garden, grounds, the interior of the church spruced up. He finally arrived with his entourage, his Catholicosal staff in hand, the knob of which glittered with many colored gems, while the church bell chimed its melodious welcome. Mass, according to the music by Ekmalian, celebrated by the Catholicos. The church, filled to capacity with the faithful, including the upper room always reserved for the women, permeated with incense, aglow with chandeliers, oil lamps, candles. The heavenly, overpowering music—*sourp, sourp* ("holy, holy")! The procession. The Catholicosal throne that He adorned—seen by me for the first and last time . . .

Such churches dotted every city and town of Turkey, because they were there before Europe heard the name "Turk." Eighty percent of major business activity in the city stopped on Sundays, because they were owned by Armenians. And this infuriated the

Turks, especially the newly appointed mayor, one Jevded Bey, who had been transferred from the city of Van. To express his displeasure, he had almost gouged out my father's eyes with his fingers.

On June 24, 1914, Archduke Francis Ferdinand was assassinated at Sarajevo and World War I was on. Turkey, ever the relentless aggressor, joined the Central Powers and soon began to execute its fiendish plans to exterminate the Armenian people. A reign of terror began throughout Turkey. There were hangings of Armenians on trumped-up charges in every nook and corner, beatings and inhuman tortures became the norm.

I have seen many such hangings in prominent squares of Marash with my own eyes . . . My father was called to the city hall three times in one night to identify decapitated heads of Armenians . . .

In early April, 1915, the deportations began in our part of the country. *Memoir of Naim Bey* records some of the day-to-day directives transmitted in code by the Ottoman government in Constantinople to various officials in the field, to make this ghastly venture a complete success.

Watching my beloved Zeytoonite and other villagers with their cattle, sheep and goats, trudge to the inns at the southern part of the city, was a searing experience that I can never, never forget. All were headed to unknown and constantly changing destinations—to central Anatolia, to Syria, to Palestine, to the burning deserts of Mesopotamia. Hunger and pestilence took its toll: Some had to graze for sustenance, like sheep and cattle.

Then a glimpse of hope. British General Sir Edmund Allenby smashed, in Palestine, the Seventh Ottoman Army Commanded by Mustafa Kemal. And the Armenians of the Legion d'Orient earned the following tribute from General Allenby: "I am proud to have had an Armenian contingent under my command. They have fought brilliantly and have played a great part in the victory."

An Anglo-Indian cavalry regiment reached Marash on

February 22, 1919. There was a tumultuous welcome and parade by the Armenians. Their five and a half centuries of subjugation was coming to an end. To quote Leonidas: "We shall be free . . . " I walked tall and proud. The Armenian tricolor—red, blue, and orange—had been resurrected in eastern Armenia at the foot of Mt. Ararat, on May 28, 1918. And the survivors of the first genocide of the twentieth century gradually began to return to their homes, mostly to Cilicia.

But soon the usual allied rivalries and intrigues reared their ugly heads. Who shall control what area? Italy occupied the seaport of Antalya in southern Anatolia. Greece had plans to liberate western Anatolia, and so on and so forth.

By the end of the year, the British occupation was replaced by the French, who began to accupy the British positions. These included the main armory, the Marash Theological Seminary, the Latin monastery, and various other Armenian churches, orphanages, and certain inns. The troops, well over five thousand, consisted of the French, Armenian Legionnaires, Senegalese, Algerians, and some others.

The Turks revolted against French rule in January 1920, which lasted three weeks. It was the very first Kemalist move against Allied occupation. A fair account of this episode is given by the late Stanley E. Kerr in his *The Lions of Marash,* and Gh. Chorbajian's *Memoirs* of the events and the conflict appearing in the spring 1979 issue of the *Armenian Review.*

> At a given signal, the Turks began to fire at French positions and Armenian houses. The massacre of the defenseless had begun—a centuries-old Turkish habit—yet once more. I found myself in our church, St. Stephen's, with some relatives and a half a hundred others, at the foot of the northern part of the citadel. We were completely defenseless.
>
> On the other hand, there was a strong garrison at the walled, impregnable Latin monastery, built on a prominent hill that dominated the area. They were

but a mile east of us; I could see the four-story rectangular bell tower, which had become a machine gun nest, from the little window over one of our church's minor altars (all Armenian churches face east, a reminder of our sun-worshipping ancestors). If only we could get there somehow. But how? And the machine gun kept singing its monotonous song, ra-ta-ta; ra-ta-ta . . .

The Turks began setting Armenian houses afire all over the city. They now approached our church. There was no time to lose. We could not leave through the main door, since the building across the street quartered a company of Turkish irregulars, well armed. So a number of us built a makeshift ladder from of a funeral bier and slipped out the rear of the church at midnight on a very dark night. In order to forestall detection, we removed our shoes and proceeded in our stocking feet. It was the fifth night of the conflict. Undetected, we reached our home in a short time, about a mile to the south. We descended to the house from the flat roof in the rear.

My grandfather, in his mid-seventies and paralyzed on the left side, inquired about my father and the rest of the family with gestures of his right hand. All I knew was that they had gone on the first day of the conflict, to visit parishioners whose home was not far from the Latin monastery. Sophia, a neighbor, had been feeding grandfather.

On the second night we received signals from Armenian neighbors from across the street. They had noticed our arrival and invited us to their quarters. We were glad to join them. That night I had my first restful sleep in many a day. In the middle of the night I was suddenly awakened. An Armenian commando had come from the monastery and had advised us to seek refuge there. Again, there was no time to lose. We knew full well the dangers we would be confronting in the process.

67

There was no way we could take grandpa along with us. Call it cowardice! My premonition was that I would never see him alive again, nor Sophia,—which proved to be the case. Yet the plain fact was that we had to pass by certain Turkish houses, all defended by well-armed men at peepholes. Better than double time would be needed to chance the hazardous passage. As it turned out, we had to tread over dead bodies. Miraculously, we overcame the first hurdle. Then there was the stretch of road along the creek, the other side of which was also fortified by the Turks. And the steep hill to the top. As we ran full steam ahead, a hail of enemy bullets whizzed about our heads and bodies. Fortunately for us, this was before the advent of infrared technology. At long last we reached the summit, protected by a wall, breathless . . . and all accounted for. As we caught our collective breath, we shouted "Armenien! Armenien!" The guards searched us for weapons, there admitted us to the compound. Soon I rejoined the rest of the family, who had taken refuge in the monastery with our friends. Oh, it felt so safe here!

A multitude of us—men, women and children—huddled together, spent the night in the church proper, slept or dozed off as best we could. In the middle of the night, I was startled to hear the thunderous ra-ta-ta of a machine gun in the upper room being fired at Turkish positions.

The following morning, I was detailed to carry bricks to the bell tower. The captain of the garrison had decided to put up walls in the huge circular windows, having lost several machine gunners to Turkish sharpshooters' fire. From the fourth floor of the tower I could see the very top of the citadel, to the west, flat, its northern side completely dominated by our vantage point. Then a volley of bullets hit the tower, and a ricochetting bullet fragment got my right eye. When I woke up on a cot some hours later I found Dr. Avedis attending me.

Because his house was very close to the monastery, he had access to his home clinic.

Before the work on the tower was completed, one more Armenian was killed: my classmate, Aram, had been felled previously by a dum-dum bullet. Meanwhile, escapees brought news of orphans immolated, pregnant women bayonetted—the usual tactics, rape, murder and plunder, for which the Turks have been infamous for ten centuries . . .

The tenth day of the conflict was cold. Dark clouds overhung the city. With his binoculars, Abbot Mure could see intense, hectic activity in the church of St. Asdvadsadzin on the hill to the southwest of the city. Large Red Cross signs appeared on the roof. The fifty Armenian legionnaires had exhausted all their ammunition and were completely helpless. Couriers with urgent appeals for help had been sent to the major in charge of the French troops in the church of the Forty Sainted Youths, all eight hundred of them to the south of the city.

The church bell at St. Asdvadsadzin began to broadcast a slow, mournful, dirge, *ding-dong, ding-dong, ding-dong,* which would easily be heard at the church of the Forty Sainted Youths . . . The Turks had saturated the roofs of the school building and the church with kerosene. *Ding-dong . . . Ding-dong . . .*

Hear the loud alarm bells
Brazen bells!
What a tale of terror, now their turbulency tells!
In the startled ear of day
How they scream out their affright!
Much too horrified to speak,
They can only shriek, shriek,
How the danger sinks and swells,
By the sinking or the swelling in the anger of the bells . . .
Of the bells—
Of the bells, bells, bells,

69

Bells, bells, bells—
In the clamor and clanging of the bells!

Soon dark smoke gathered in the church area. Then tiny specks of light could be seen, becoming brighter and brighter with each passing moment. Then the entire area was aglow with reddish light. The bell had stopped tolling many minutes before . . .

Thus, two thousand innocent Armenians of all ages and both sexes joined their maker, from an earthly Inferno that had been His church . . .

And the "chivalrous" French would not lift a finger to help them.

It is an irony of fate, *kismet,* that a French column, with important artillery units, arrived several days later from Adana, the capital of Cilicia, and camped on the plateau a short distance west of St. Asdvadsadzin Church. Then they began to pound the Turkish strongholds in the city, mosques and minarets included. And Armenian freedom fighters in the northeastern part of the city subdued the entire area; their advance units reached the monastery unhindered.

A French plane arrived and dropped packages to the French positions. The Turks were completely demoralized. The Armenian band in the monastery played the Marseillaise amid general jubilation. That was the twenty-first day of the conflict. By that night, perhaps a hundred Turkish fighters were still in the city. The rest had fled in panic to the villages to the north and east of the city. The first serious attempt of Mustafa Kemal and his underlings in the city and its vicinity had failed miserably.

That same night, General Quérette of the French forces had given orders—on whose authority no one now seems to know—to his troops to retreat, leaving the Armenians without an adequate supply of arms and ammunition, since the French never armed them, to the tender mercies of the Turks. Learning of this, the Turks soon returned to the city. Thus, defeat turned into victory for the Turks, paving the way for the Smyrna debacle in late 1922, all with the connivance of the Allied powers and their direct or indirect help.

The retreat to Adana, about a hundred miles to the southwest, turned out to be extremely difficult, not only for the French troops, but particularly for the thousands of Armenians who followed them, because of hunger, the unusually cold weather and severe snow storms, many, many hundreds froze to death on the way.

On July 20, 1974, defenseless Cyprus was invaded by Turkish troops. Indiscriminate bombings, killings, kidnappings and rapes followed. The same age-old habits. The Melkonian Institute was severely damaged.

From time immemorial a Greek island, Cyprus was soon to become another target of Turkish expansionism. Little had I realized, at the time, the real meaning of General Ibrahim's message at Ft. Monmouth: "Let's attack the enemy." I had thought that he referred to the USSR, since they had had wars with them at least a baker's dozen times, usually on the losing side. The Turkish soldier has a healthy respect for his Russian counterpart. Many Turkish soldiers can recite the following, which is part of a Turkish poem:

> *When the Russian artilleryman*
> *Fires his cannonball,*
> *The earth and heaven*
> *Echo its thunder!*

The invasion of Cyprus was made possible by America's generosity, of course. Warships, transports, rifles, jeeps, tanks, machine guns, uniforms, helmets, shoes, ammunition—all were made in the USA. Before the Turkish troops reached the vicinity of St. Magar's, we had already left for the southern part of the island, carrying with us bare essentials. The monastery is now used as company headquarters by Turkish troops.

Today 200,000 Cypriotes are refugees, indeed exiles, in their own country . . . And President Timmy Harper continues

71

his daily preachments on "human rights" with a righteous glow on his face.

Geopolitics indeed makes strange bedfellows. One cannot help but remind oneself of the date 1853, when Emperor Louis Napoleon's army teamed up in the Crimea with that of the British sovereign, the Defender of the Faith, to fight against Russia, a Christian nation, in support of the Turkish army. Compare this with the action of King John III of Poland, who smashed the Turkish army under Kara (Black) Mustafa at the gates of Vienna in 1683, forcing them into a disorderly retreat and thus perhaps guaranteeing the continuance of a Christian Central and Eastern Europe.

I returned to the United States on August 20, 1974. In Cyprus I had relived some of the episodes of my early life in Turkey. Such is life.

CHAPTER 11

Impossible Dreams, Impossible Tasks?

It was clear to me that lawlessness was rampant in the world, even among nations that considered themselves as "civilized" and "religious." One hears of an information explosion—which is in many cases misinformation—but never of information suppression. Man has reached the point of no return, yet he still adheres to his old and deceitful ways. Invisible governments act in devious ways, and their henchmen assume a variety of postures. My recent experience in Cyprus had proved that, if additional proof were needed and it was not.

One glaring example is the deliberate and methodical ignoring of the first genocide of the twentieth century, but never the second. One wonders who makes such godlike decisions. I decided that, before I closed my eyes permanently, it would be a good idea to try to find out firsthand.

My first letter was addressed to President Larry McCord, reminding him of the first genocide of our century. His reply was disappointing and his lack of knowledge distressing. He spoke of this country's long friendship with Turkey. The actual fact is that that country had sided with the Central Powers in World War I. During World War II she remained neutral, but in favor of the Axis Powers, and was prepared to pounce on the Caucasus the minute Stalingrad fell to the Germans,

73

to realize finally her long-cherished dream of Pan-Turanism. She had a good precedent: the Allies and Japanese had taken similar action against imperial Russia after World War I.

Since the mid-1850's many hundreds of American missionaries have been stationed in Turkey, yet they have not been able to establish *one single* Turkish Christian church. In the meantime, the Turks destroyed several thousand Armenian and Greek churches, monasteries, and convents throughout the length and breadth of Turkey—the pioneers of Christian heritage in the Middle East.

President McCord is obviously unaware of George Horton's book *The Blight of Asia,*—a very apt title—which deals with the sacking and burning of Smyrna in late 1922 by the Turks. Mr. Horton, a U.S. diplomat in the Near East for thirty years, quotes from St. John's Revelations:

> What thou seest, write in a book, and send it unto the seven churches which are in Asia; unto Ephesus, and unto Smyrna, and unto Pergamos, and unto Thyatira, and unto Sardis, and unto Philadelphia, and unto Laodicea.

James W. Gerard, a former U.S. ambassador to Germany, has the following to say in his foreword to this book:

> ... that it should have been possible twenty centuries after the birth of Christ for a small and backward nation like the Turks to have committed such crimes against civilization and the progress of the world is a matter which should cause all conscientious people to pause and think.

Yet the writer shows conclusively that these crimes have been committed without opposition on the part of any Christian nation and that the last frightful scene at Smyrna was enacted within a few yards of a powerful Allied and American battle fleet.

We turned a deaf ear to the dying Christians when they called to us for aid, fully aware that America was their only hope, and now it would appear that there is a growing tendency in this country to whitewash the Turks and condone their crimes in order to obtain material advantages from them.

Fraternizing with them on any other terms creates a suspicion of sordidness or even complicity. From the outspoken nature of this book it will be evident to the reader that the writing of it has required considerable courage and that it has been inspired by no other possible motive than a desire to make the truth known about matters which it is important for the world to know.

Amen!

I next turned to our astute and erudite secretary of state, Heinrich Kissky, for a more scholarly evaluation. In a letter dated October 2, 1974, the director, office of Southern European affairs, replied as follows:

The Secretary of State has asked me to reply to your letter of July 29 asking whether the U.S. government is prepared to raise with the government of Turkey the question of compensation for actions *you state* (emphasis mine) that Turkey undertook toward its Armenian minority more than fifty years ago. We are sorry to reply so belatedly, but your letter arrived at the height of the Cyprus crisis, and we are only now catching up with our mail concerning the countries of the eastern Mediterranean.

While the department is aware of the depth of feeling among many people of Armenian descent on the matter which you raise, we do not believe there is any appropriate legal or political/diplomatic framework in which we can or should raise the question of compensation with the government of Turkey. Moreover, our doing so would, we think, be contrary to the interests of the Armenian community living in Turkey today. Etc.

The Department of State pretends to be unaware of certain facts. Furthermore, the Armenian question was first raised at the Congress of Berlin in 1878, in modern times. The words "double standard" come to mind.

I had great hopes for the country and the world when a "born-again" Christian was inaugurated president of the United States. I prayed that he would to some degree match the brilliance of a Woodrow Wilson. So I wrote the following letter on April 24, 1977, to President Timmy Harper:

Dear Mr. President:

This is an appeal to bring the unpunished and unrepentant perpetrators of the first genocide of the twentieth century before the bar of international justice, as were the Nazi criminals and Japanese warlords after World War II. This refers, of course, to the Turkish government and people, whom a former consul general of the United States, stationed in the Near East, George Horton, called "the blight of Asia." Thus far they have gotten off scot-free. Proving—if additional proof were needed—the double standard in our world society.

I was born in Marash, Cilicia, Turkey, in 1905, the son of a priest whose forebears had been priests of the Armenian Church for twenty generations. Having been an eyewitness to the tortures, unspeakable indignities, massacres and deportations, I, like thousands of Armenians in the country and throughout the world, shed my daily tears for the innocent dead. It is humanly impossible to forget, Mr. President, the heart-rending cries of two thousand men, women and children who were burned to death by Turkish barbarians in one church alone.

Today our hundreds of chapels, churches, cathedrals, convents and monasteries, many of them centuries-old architectural masterpieces, are in ruins, and others remain desecrated and are used as warehouses.

In spite of these dastardly acts, Turkey was admitted to the League of Nations after World War I, as it became a member of the United Nations after World War II. As you can see, Mr. President, these acts speak volumes about our twentieth century civilizations.

It is most gratifying for this citizen to bring to your attention portions of a letter that that great American, President Woodrow Wilson of Fourteen Points fame, wrote to an Armenian leader in Paris in 1919, expressing his most sincere and outspoken sympathy for the Armenian cause, and concluding his words with "the warmest friendliness for the Armenian people to whom my sympathy goes out most heartily."

When, about ten centuries ago, two Turkish tribes left their abodes in Central Asia and headed westward, their principal accomplishments were destruction, plunder and rape of thriving towns, cities and states already established in the area long ago.

True to form, today's Turkey, acting on flimsy pretexts, in mid 1974 invaded the Republic of Cyprus in broad daylight—Mr. President, I was an eyewitness to these events—occupying almost one half of the island, causing thousands of deaths and injuries and much destruction, while the "civilized" world stood idly—and cowardly—by.

Turks like to protect their "rights" while consistently denying the rights of others. To cite just one case, they have been flagrantly violating the rights of the minorities in Turkey, which are guaranteed by the Treaty of Lausanne. The valiant efforts of the Armenian Patriarch of Constantinople in this direction are always frustrated, and his appeals to higher authority fall on deaf ears . . .

The Turks deny even the existence of millions of Kurds in the country, a distinct Aryan race with its own Indo-European language.

Mr. President, a peaceful world must be a just world.

Respectfully yours,
A Survivor

This letter, too, unfortunately did not achieve any positive results.

Then I turned to that venerable, fearless and indomitable champion of freedom and justice throughout the universe, the *New York Times,* for help, nor was this a first attempt. On May 8, 1977, I wrote to its editorial board the following:

Gentlemen:

On April 4 you published a column by G. Hamburger dealing with the Turkish-Armenian question. The following day I mailed to you a letter dealing with this topic. Since then, not a single letter has appeared in your paper regarding the aforesaid column. It is impossible to imagine that none was received by you.

One must conclude, then, that you are exercising censorship as to who shall—and shall not—be heard on this grave question. Your arrogance of power obviously matches that of a Hitler or Stalin. I urge you to publish my letter, since no power on earth can still this Armenian's voice. Here it is.

I have read with much interest G. Hamburger's column of April 9, wherein he offers some useful and thoughtful suggestions. But I must take strong exception to his statement about "what the Armenians call this century's first genocide." Not so. Not only the Armenians; for we read the following lines in Dr. Ralph Elliott Cook's doctoral dissertation, dated April 15, 1957, entitled "The United States and the Armenian Question, 1894-1924." "There is much evidence that the deportations were merely vehicles upon which to base an official policy of genocide—unparalled in scope in modern history with the exception of the anti-Semitic program of Nazi Germany."

Further, we read in the late Dr. Stanley E. Kerr's book: "The dissident member of the Ittihad, Mevlan Zade Rifat, charged that the deportations were actually planned by the Young Turk committee as a means of solving the

78

Armenian question by genocide," and he quotes suggestions made in the comittee meetings for accomplishing this purpose.

Talaat and Enver admitted their intentions to the American ambassador to Constantinople, Henry Morgenthau, when we protested against the inhuman treatment of the Armenians. Finally, records of the postwar courts martial of Turkish officials by Turkish courts confirm the guilt of the Ittihad and its leaders, and make reference to the following: "Among the judgments rendered by Turkish courts martial are (a) those of 27 April and 10 July 1919, in which Talaat, Enver and Jamal pashas were found guilty and condemned to death for deporting and massacring the Armenian people . . . "

Finally, may I bring to Mr. Sulzberger's attention the Minority Rights Group's Report No 32, published in London, entitled "The Armenians," which the *Guardian* calls "an able and comprehensive account."

Space does not allow the mere listing of such other countless competent accounts.

Respectfully,
A Survivor

This letter, as is their wont, was duly ignored by the *Times*.

In desperation, I turned to a spiritual leader for real help. I mailed the following letter to Pope Paul VI on May 22, 1977:

Your Holiness:

It was with considerable dismay that I recently learned that the state of Vatican City maintains diplomatic relations with Turkey. The reason for this, Your Holiness, is a simple one, as will be seen below.

I am sure, Your Holiness, that you are well aware of the centuries-old policy of oppression, suppression, and extermination that Turkey has pursued, particularly as regards its Christian minorities, that culminated in the first genocide of the twentieth century, that perpetrated on the Armenian people. I do know whereof I speak, Your Holiness, since I was an eyewitness to those terrible, revolting and inhuman events.

The Turks remain unpunished and unrepentant. And they continue their barbarisms unchecked. Witness, as a mere example, their recent rape of the Republic of Cyprus.

Of course, the so-called Christian nations of Europe and the Americas, and others, have diplomatic relations with Turkey. But their primary reasons are to curry favor for strategic and/or economic considerations, and unfortunately, little else.

Your Holiness, who shall speak for the weak and unprotected, for universal peace with justice for all? I sincerely hope that you will make your voice heard.

Prayerfully yours,
A Survivor

I received the following curt note from Washington, postmarked June 3, 1977, on the stationery of the Secretariat of State, The Vatican, dated May 28, 1977:

Dear—
I am directed to acknowledge the letter which you recently addressed to the Holy Father and to assure you that the contents have been noted
With good wishes, I remain
Sincerely yours,
Assessor

Since I consider this note sacrilegious and blasphemous, I must withhold any extended comment. The Pope is ten years my senior, and the information alluded to is, to coin a phrase, at his fingertips.

80

Diplomats and statesmen are expected to be slippery, but the Pope ... the apogee of piety and human rectitude? Is it any wonder, then, that the world is in such a mess?

Being a persistent character, I then appealed to the secretary general of the United Nations, with a letter dated June 5, 1977.

Dear Mr. Waldheim:

I am writing this letter to protest the membership of Turkey in the United Nations. Because it does not deserve such membership. History clearly shows that Turkey—the original two tribes from Central Asia— has been and continues to be a gangster nation, unpunished and unrepentant.

In 1932 I wrote Secretary General Salvador de Madariaga of the League of Nations, urging him to deny membership to Turkey in that organization, since it had perpetrated the first genocide of the twentieth century on the Armenians during World War I. (I am a survivor.) International morality being what it was—and is—Turkey was admitted to that organization.

Mr. Secretary General, since you have firsthand information about the Turkish barbarisms, such as the one going on presently on Cyprus, I deem additional documentation superfluous.

May I remind you respectfully that only a just and effective United Nations can perpetuate itself.

Yours very truly,
H. H. H.

For weeks I waited for a reply. Obviously, after being duly noted by an underling, my letter was deposited in the round file. In a very last effort, I turned to the editor of the *World Almanac & Book of Facts*. He responded graciously with the following letter:

Dear—

There is no doubt of a 22-year history (1894-1915) of Ottoman brutality against the Armenian people, beginning with the massacres under Abdul Hamid in 1894 and culminating in the "final solution" of the 1915 "deportations."

We are planning major revisions in our Memorable Dates section next year (the 1979 edition) and will, I hope, be able to include this information at that time.

Sincerely,
G. E. D., Editor

It was gratifying to learn that there are still honest and free Americans who can call a genocidist a genocidist.

When one puts such bare facts before presidents or secretaries of state and others, they seem to look at you askance for bringing up such stupid questions—for very transparent reasons. Professing the highest of ideals, they seem actually to practice the morality of the underworld. We, humans—for want of a better term—inhabit this jungle world, in which invisible "governments," with designs of their own, pose a real if invisible threat to life in every form.

Like yesteryear's "cultural revolution" in China, a sexual revolution is in full swing here. Big deal! And business as usual seems to be the common mood.

Precious few seem to realize the full meaning of the phrase, "The genie is out of the bottle."

CHAPTER 12

Adieu, Paradise

Tick-tock, tick-tock, tick-tock . . .

The time has come for me to take stock of my life and give credit where it is due. Almost six decades ago my family sought asylum here from the barbaric land of Turkey (the Turk is the same old Turk, whether he is called Seljuk, Ottoman, or Kemalist-Republican Turk) and Uncle Sam opened his doors to us, for which my belated but humble thanks. To this day, our safety and lives have never been threatened. Our aim has been to become *good* citizens. Whether or not we have succeeded is not for me to say.

I have written quite a bit on a matter that concerns me very much—the Armenian cause—and no one has told me to stop doing so.

But during the past quarter of a century, the complexities of life have taken a quantum jump. English, a very rich language, is misused and abused. Suddenly, "invasion" becomes "incursion." Two thousand years ago, Jesus, whip in hand, chased the money changers from the temple. Today there is an excellent opportunity for a bright, enterprising person to do the same with the word changers.

Four words have become fetishes: "national interest" and "national security." Think tanks' and computers' projections abound.

The other day I received an invitation from the Department of the Army, HQ, U.S. Army Recruiting Command, Fort Sheridan, Illinois 60037, inviting me to join the army. And of course "the army takes care of its own." My age is three score and ten plus. Computers, anyone?

More often than not, one fears the control of powerful and selfish and greedy men interested in profits only. Pimps in Ph.D. guise are not hard to find.

Nuclear weapons are coming out of our ears, our stockpiles are overflowing, yet we—and our supposed enemy, the USSR—produce more with each passing day. What we already have on hand can incinerate the entire globe and all living things several times over. Yet we have the temerity to preach righteously to others not to do the same thing: "You see the mote in your brother's eye, but not the beam in yours."

Warmongers seem to be in charge in high places and endure that we must, as we endured the inglorious reign of a J. Edgar Hoover, for whom the socialists were devils incarnate to be treated accordingly.

I have complete confidence in my representative in the Congress, above all in his integrity. But the invisible government seems to be in a position to befuddle the most competent and dedicated of presidents. And the general public is a fun-loving mass that couldn't care less.

The Supreme Puppeteer in His infinite wisdom never whispers to the newborn babe the number of his or her allotted days or years . . . So I have decided to return to the Land of Ararat, the reborn Armenia, where my roots are. I will visit the glorious capital city of Yerevan and enjoy the beauty of Lake Sevan. For the first time I will observe the twin snow-capped peaks of Mt. Ararat, which Noah's Ark made so famous, and which is so unjustly held by Turkey.

Then I will visit Yerevan's park, the Citadel of Swallows, where stands the somber, stark and austere Memorial Monument erected to memorialize the first genocide of the twentieth century; I will shed my tears at the "Eternal Flame . . . "

84

The cussedness and barbarity of human nature has no bounds.

I shall live in the monastery of St. Etchmiadzin (the word means "where the Only Begotten Son descended"). A mere ten miles from Yerevan lies the seat of the Supreme Patriarch and Catholicos of All Armenians, where I am assured adequate living quarters.

Good-bye, Yervant!

Thank you, America, for many favors. And adieu.

And the genie is out of the bottle.

Tick-tock, tick-tock, tick-tock . . .

B HAIG, H.
Haig, H   H
Return to Mount Ararat :
or the education of Nshan:
a living novel

		DATE DUE		